HIPPOCRENE

GW01457847

BEGINNER'S
JAPANESE
WITH 2 AUDIO CDs

SECOND EDITION

Joanne Redmond

HIPPOCRENE BOOKS, INC.
New York

For my beloved Lee and Adeline. I still cannot believe God has given you to me.

Second Edition, 2013

ISBNs of previous edition: 978-0-7818-1141-4 / 0-7818-1141-4

For information, address:
HIPPOCRENE BOOKS, INC.
171 Madison Avenue
New York, NY 10016
www.hippocrenebooks.com

Cataloging-in-Publication Data is available from the Library of Congress.

ISBN-13: 978-0-7818-1327-3
ISBN-10: 0-7818-1327-1

Printed in the United States of America.

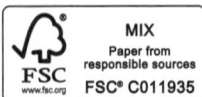

TABLE OF CONTENTS

INTRODUCTION

"You want to study Japanese? Isn't that one of the most difficult languages to learn?"

No.

Believe it or not, learning Japanese is not as hard as you might think. While mastering a language is an ongoing process, it generally takes the average Japanese person five to eight years to become fluent in English, while only two to three years for an English-speaking individual to become proficient in Japanese.

PURPOSE OF THIS BOOK

This book is designed to equip you with a solid foundation of Japanese conversation. As with many languages, Japanese contains various levels of social language. This book will focus on verbiage that is acceptable to all levels of society.

This text provides the foundation for a strong grasp of Japanese conversation and grammar structure and the skills to read *hiragana* and *katakana*, two of the Japanese phonetic alphabets.

BOOK STRUCTURE

DIALOGUES

Dialogues are written in *hiragana* and *katakana*, followed by *rōmaji* and translated into English. Try to read *hiragana* and *katakana* as often as possible. Practice dialogues with another partner, preferably a Japanese person. The dialogues are based on everyday conversations.

VOCABULARY

New terms are introduced in every dialogue and defined in each chapter. Additional words taught in the lesson are included. Memorize all vocabulary terms and note the use of each in sentences.

COLUMNS

Special notes are located in columns on the right pages of each chapter. This section explains complex words, phrases and articles. It also includes cultural information and other useful tips.

GRAMMAR EXPLANATION

New grammar concepts are explained in this area. Examples are given for clarification.

EXERCISES

Here you will practice drills to develop vocabulary and grammar skills. It is important to master this section before moving to the next chapter because the lessons build on each other.

SHORT DIALOGUES

Short dialogues are given for practice, enabling you to adapt your conversations when words or phrases are slightly altered.

SELF-TEST

This section allows you to test yourself and insure you understand the words and concepts in each lesson. Answers are located on page 251.

DIFFERENCES BETWEEN JAPANESE AND ENGLISH

- Most publications read from top to bottom, right to left.

- There are no spaces between words or characters.

- Verb conjugation is the same regardless of gender, number or person of the subject. This reduces much difficulty in learning the language.

- Plurals are rarely used.

- Adjectives are changed to reflect past tense and negatives.

- There is no future tense.

- People typically speak in a monotone, rarely inflecting their voices.

JAPANESE WRITING AND PRONUNCIATION

The Japanese have three methods of writing: *Hiragana*, *katakana* and *kanji*. *Rōmaji*, Japanese characters translated into the English alphabet, was created shortly after World War II.

HIRAGANA is a phonetic alphabet taught to kindergarten students. The name of each letter is the same as its pronunciation, unlike English, where pronunciation is different from the letter names.

KATAKANA is also a phonetic alphabet used for foreign words. For example, terms like *McDonald's, elevator* and *Christmas* would be written in *katakana*.

KANJI are Chinese characters that represent pictures instead of sounds. For example, 木 = tree.

RŌMAJI consists of Japanese words written in the English alphabet and is rarely found in publications. However, you will see *rōmaji* printed on signs in various Japanese tourists spots and in train stations.

Hiragana, *katakana* and *kanji* are often used together in one sentence:

I ate ice cream. 私はアイスクリームを食べました.

Hiragana = は, を, べました

Katakana = アイスクリーム

Kanji = 私, 食

HIRAGANA

If you master this phonetic alphabet, you can speak any word in Japanese with nearly native pronunciation. Unlike English letters, these characters represent one sound only, with the exception of *n*. Further, every sound used in *hiragana*, and therefore every sound in Japanese, is one familiar to English-speaking individuals. This makes pronunciation quite simple.

Every character receives an equal beat in each word.

あ **a** like **a** in **water**

い **i** like **e** in **feet**

う **u** like **u** in **flute**, with the lips spread instead of rounded

え **e** like **e** in **egg**

お **o** like **o** in **ghost**

i and **u** are often voiceless when preceded by **k, t, p, s, shi, h** or **f**.

a, i, u, e and **o** maintain the same sound when paired with a consonant.

か **ka**　き **ki**　く **ku**　け **ke**　こ **ko**
The **k** is like **k** in **kite**.

が **ga**　ぎ **gi**　ぐ **gu**　げ **ge**　ご **go**
The **g** sound is like **g** in **goat**.

さ **sa**　し **shi**　す **su**　せ **se**　そ **so**
Shi is pronounced the same as the English word **she**. The remaining consonants are like the **s** in **song**.

ざ **za**   じ **ji**   ず **zu**   ぜ **ze**   ぞ **zo**
The **z** is like the **z** in **zoo**. The **j** is like the **j** in **joke**.

た **ta**   ち **chi**   つ **tsu**   て **te**   と **to**
The **t** is like the **t** in **talk**. **Chi** is like **chee** in **cheese**, but without extending the vowel sound. **Tsu** is like the **tsu** in **Mitsubishi**.

だ **da**   ぢ **ji**   づ **zu**   で **de**   ど **do**
The **d** is like the **d** in **dog**. Note that the *ji* and *zu* here are not as commonly used as the *ji* and *zu* at the top of the page.

な **na**   に **ni**   ぬ **nu**   ね **ne**   の **no**
The **n** is like the **n** in **nice**.

は **ha**   ひ **hi**   ふ **fu**   へ **he**   ほ **ho**
The **h** is like the **h** in **hat**. The **f** sounds like a combination of the English **h** and f. The lips do not touch the teeth. The sound is similar to that of blowing out a candle, though not as strong. The lips are slightly parted without being rounded.

ば **ba**   び **bi**   ぶ **bu**   べ **be**   ぼ **bo**
The **b** is like the **b** in **ball**.

ぱ **pa**   ぴ **pi**   ぷ **pu**   ぺ **pe**   ぽ **po**
The **p** is like the **p** in **pipe**.

ま **ma**   み **mi**   む **mu**   め **me**   も **mo**
The **m** is like the **m** in **man**.

や **ya**   ゆ **yu**   よ **yo**
The **y** is like the **y** in **yellow**.

ら **ra**   り **ri**   る **ru**   れ **re**   ろ **ro**
The **r** sound is a combination of the English **l** and **r**. The tongue quickly touches the top of the mouth just behind the teeth.

わ **wa**
The **w** sound is like the **w** in **water**, but a little more relaxed.

ん **n**
The **n** sound varies, depending on where it is located within a word.

- Preceding **b, p** or **m**, it is like **m** in **may**.

- Preceding **z, t, d** or **n**, it is like **n** in **new**.

- Preceding **k, g,** or **n** (ん), it is like **ng** in **sing**, without pronouncing the final **g** sound.

ya, **yu** and **yo** can replace **i** after all characters that are paired with an **i**.

きゃ **kya**	きゅ **kyu**	きょ **kyo**
ぎゃ **gya**	ぎゅ **gyu**	ぎょ **gyo**
しゃ **sha**	しゅ **shu**	しょ **sho**
じゃ **ja**	じゅ **ju**	じょ **jo**
ちゃ **cha**	ちゅ **chu**	ちょ **cho**
にゃ **nya**	にゅ **nyu**	にょ **nyo**
ひゃ **hya**	ひゅ **hyu**	ひょ **hyo**
びゃ **bya**	びゅ **byu**	びょ **byo**
ぴゃ **pya**	ぴゅ **pyu**	ぴょ **pyo**
みゃ **mya**	みゅ **myu**	みょ **myo**
りゃ **rya**	りゅ **ryu**	りょ **ryo**

DOUBLE VOWELS

Vowel sounds are never blended. If two of the same vowel occur successively, simply extend the vowel sound an additional beat.

ああ	ā	held for two beats
いい	ii	held for two beats
うう	ū	held for two beats
ええ	ē	held for two beats
おお	ō	held for two beats

Examples:

おばさん	*obasan*	aunt
おばあさん	*obāsan*	grandmother
います	*imasu*	exist, be
いいます	*iimasu*	say
おき	*Oki*	girl's name
おおきい	*ōkii*	big

DOUBLE CONSONANTS

When a small っ appears in a word, the consonant directly after it receives an extra beat. Do not repeat the consonant twice, but pause briefly before saying the consonant.

いた	*ita*	exist
いった	*itta*	went

PARTICLES

は	*wa*	denotes subject
を	*o*	follows an object
へ	*e*	indicates direction

STUDY HINTS

- Try to study a little every day. You will learn much more this way than if you studied for long periods of time intermittently.

- Try to meet with a Japanese person or fluent Japanese speaker at least once a week.

- Do not move on to the next lesson until you have mastered the current one.

- Do not deviate from the correct pronunciation described previously.

- Try to incorporate Japanese terms and phrases into your daily life. Speak and think in Japanese as much as possible.

Ganbatte kudasai!

Good luck!

HIRAGANA

あ a	い i	う u	え e	お o
か ka	き ki	く ku	け ke	こ ko
さ sa	し shi	す su	せ se	そ so
た ta	ち chi	つ tsu	て te	と to
な na	に ni	ぬ nu	ね ne	の no
は ha	ひ hi	ふ fu	へ he	ほ ho
ま ma	み mi	む mu	め me	も mo
や ya		ゆ yu		よ yo
ら ra	り ri	る ru	れ re	ろ ro
わ wa				を o
が ga	ぎ gi	ぐ gu	げ ge	ご go
ざ za	じ ji	ず zu	ぜ ze	ぞ zo
だ da	ぢ ji	づ zu	で de	ど do
ば ba	び bi	ぶ bu	べ be	ぼ bo
ぱ pa	ぴ pi	ぷ pu	ぺ pe	ぽ po
きゃ kya		きゅ kyu		きょ kyo
しゃ sha		しゅ shu		しょ sho
ちゃ cha		ちゅ chu		ちょ cho
にゃ nya		にゅ nyu		にょ nyo
ひゃ hya		ひゅ hyu		ひょ hyo
みゃ mya		みゅ myu		みょ myo
りゃ rya		りゅ ryu		りょ ryo
ぎゃ gya		ぎゅ gyu		ぎょ gyo
じゃ ja		じゅ ju		じょ jo
びゃ bya		びゅ byu		びょ byo
ぴゃ pya		ぴゅ pyu		ぴょ pyo
ん n				

KATAKANA

ア a	イ i	ウ u	エ e	オ o
カ ka	キ ki	ク ku	ケ ke	コ ko
サ sa	シ shi	ス su	セ se	ソ so
タ ta	チ chi	ツ tsu	テ te	ト to
ナ na	ニ ni	ヌ nu	ネ ne	ノ no
ハ ha	ヒ hi	フ fu	ヘ he	ホ ho
マ ma	ミ mi	ム mu	メ me	モ mo
ヤ ya		ユ yu		ヨ yo
ラ ra	リ ri	ル ru	レ re	ロ ro
ワ wa				ヲ o
ガ ga	ギ gi	グ gu	ゲ ge	ゴ go
ザ za	ジ ji	ズ zu	ゼ ze	ゾ zo
ダ da	ヂ ji	ヅ zu	デ de	ド do
バ ba	ビ bi	ブ bu	ベ be	ボ bo
パ pa	ピ pi	プ pu	ペ pe	ポ po
キャ kya		キュ kyu		キョ kyo
シャ sha		シュ shu		ショ sho
チャ cha		チュ chu		チョ cho
ニャ nya		ニュ nyu		ニョ nyo
ヒャ hya		ヒュ hyu		ヒョ hyo
ミャ mya		ミュ myu		ミョ myo
リャ rya		リュ ryu		リョ ryo
ギャ gya		ギュ gyu		ギョ gyo
ジャ ja		ジュ ju		ジョ jo
ビャ bya		ビュ byu		ビョ byo
ピャ pya		ピュ pyu		ピョ pyo
ン n				

LESSON ONE
IMA NANJI DESU-KA

In this lesson you will learn:

- Basic sentence formation
- How to tell time
- Numbers one through one hundred

DIALOGUE

I

A: すみません。とけいを もって いますか。

B: はい。

A: いま なんじ ですか。

B: はちじ はん です。

A: ありがとう ございます。

B: どう いたしまして。

II

たなか: ジョンソンさん、あなたの でんわ ばんごうを おしえて ください。

ジョンソン: はい。わたしの でんわ ばんごうは ろく に いち の きゅう なな ご さん です。

たなか: ありがとう ございます。

I

A: *Sumimasen, tokei-o motte imasu-ka.*

B: *Hai.*

A: *Ima nanji desu-ka.*

B: *Hachiji-han desu.*

A: *Arigatō gozaimasu.*

B: *Dō itashimashite.*

II

Tanaka: *Jonson-san, anata-no denwa bangō-o oshiete kudasai.*

Jonson: *Hai. Watashi-no denwa bangō-wa roku ni ichi no kyū nana go san desu.*

T: *Arigatō gozaimasu.*

I

A: Excuse me, do you have a watch?

B: Yes.

A: What time is it?

B: It is eight thirty.

A: Thank you very much.

B: You are welcome.

II

Tanaka: Mr. Johnson, please tell me your telephone number.

Johnson: Sure. My telephone number is 621-9753.

T: Thank you very much.

GRAMMAR EXPLANATION
1. Wa

Wa is always added to the subject of every sentence. However, in the Hiragana alphabet, one does not use the symbol わ, instead は is used.

> *ex.* とうきょう**は** いま ろくじ です。
>
> *Tōkyō-**wa** ima roku-ji desu.*
> In Tokyo, it is 6:00.

The basic sentence structure in Japanese is:

> Subject-**wa** object verb.

2. Ka

Ka changes a sentence from a statement to a question. It is used at the end of a sentence.

> *ex. Yoji desu.*   It is 4:00.
> *Yoji desu-**ka**.*   Is it 4:00?

3. Nani

Nani means "what." *Nani* can be combined with the word following it by dropping the final *i*. For example, "What is it?" in Japanese is said ***nan***desu-ka, or "what time?" becomes ***nan**ji*.

4. Ban

To state "number one, number two," etc., combine the number with *ban*.

> *ex. ichi**ban***   number one
> *ni**ban***   number two

Han

Han is used in telling time when saying it is half-past something.

Gozaimasu

Gozaimasu is a polite word added to phrases like "thank you" and "good morning." It does not change the meaning of the word, it simply adds respect.

-San

-San is used at the end of people's first or last names. It is similar to saying "Mr." or "Ms." Whenever you speak to or about a Japanese individual, you should use *-san*. However, when referring to yourself, or introducing yourself, *-san* should not be used.

anata
you

arigatō
thank you

asa
morning

ban
number

denwa
telephone

denwa bangō
telephone number

desu
is

dō itashi-mashite
you are welcome

dōmo arigatō
thank you very much

gogo
p.m.

gozen
a.m.

hai
yes

han
half

iie
no

ima
now

EXERCISES

1. Memorize numbers 1 - 12:

1	*ichi*	7	*shichi, nana*
2	*ni*	8	*hachi*
3	*san*	9	*kyū*
4	*shi, yon*	10	*jū*
5	*go*	11	*jūichi*
6	*roku*	12	*jūni*

2. Add *ji* to each number to express the time:

ex. 1:00 - *ichiji*   2:00 - *niji*, etc.

1:00 -	7:00 -
2:00 -	8:00 -
3:00 -	9:00 -
4:00 -	10:00 -
5:00 -	11:00 -
6:00 -	12:00 -

3. Add *ji* and *han* to each number to express half-past:

ex. 1:30 - *ichiji-han*   2:30 - *niji-han, etc.*

1:30 -	7:30 -
2:30 -	8:30 -
3:30 -	9:30 -
4:30 -	10:30 -
5:30 -	11:30 -
6:30 -	12:30 -

4

4. Use each number in a sentence to state the time:

ex. 1:00, 1:30

➡ *Ima **ichiji** desu.*

➡ *Ima **ichiji-han** desu.*

1:00 -	7:00 -
2:30 -	8:30 -
3:00 -	9:00 -
4:30 -	10:30 -
5:00 -	11:00 -
6:30 -	12:30 -

5. Practice saying "The party's from _____ until _____" by substituting the times found below into the underlined sections:

ex. 4:00, 6:00

➡ *Pātī-wa **yoji** kara **rokuji** made desu.*

2:00, 5:00	1:00, 10:00
7:00, 8:00	11:00, 3:00
12:00, 2:00	9:00, 11:00
3:00, 6:00	4:00, 7:00
5:00, 10:00	

Yo, Ku
When telling time, use *yo* for 4 and *ku* for 9.

Ji
In English, "o'clock" is only said when referring to a time directly on the hour. However, in Japanese, *ji* is always used whenever telling time after the hour is stated, then *han* or the minutes are said.

ji
time

-ka
added to
the end of
sentences
to form a
question

kara
from

kudasai
please

made
until

motte imasu
have, carry

nani
what

-no
shows
possession

-o
denotes
sentence
object

oshiete
kudasai
please tell
me, please
teach me

pātī
party

sō desu
that's right

sumimasen
excuse me

6. Memorize numbers 13 - 20:

13 *jūsan*	17 *jūshichi*
14 *jūshi*	18 *jūhachi*
15 *jūgo*	19 *jūkyu*
16 *jūroku*	20 *nijū*

7. Learn the multiples of 10:

10 *jū*	60 *rokujū*
20 *nijū*	70 *shichijū, nanajū*
30 *sanjū*	80 *hachijū*
40 *yonjū*	90 *kyūjū*
50 *gojū*	100 *hyaku*

8. Numbers 21 through 99:

21 *nijūichi*	30 *sanjū*
22 *nijūni*	31 *sanjūichi. . .*
23 *nijūsan*	41 *yonjūichi. . .*
24 *nijūshi*	51 *gojūichi. . .*
25 *nijūgo*	61 *rokujūichi. . .*
26 *nijūroku*	71 *shichijūichi. . .*
27 *nijūshichi*	81 *hachijūichi. . .*
28 *nijūhachi*	91 *kyūjūichi. . .*
29 *nujūkyu*	99 *kyūjūkyu*

SHORT DIALOGUES
Practice these dialogues changing the underlined words:

1. On the street

ex. sanji-han

> Sumisu: *Sumimasen, ima nanji desu-ka*
> Tanaka: *Ima **sanji-han** desu.*
> Sumisu: ***Sanji-han** desu-ka.*
> Tanaka: *Sō desu.*
> Sumisu: *Arigatō gozaimasu.*
> Tanaka: *Dō itashimashite.*

1. rokuji
2. jūichiji-han
3. hachiji
4. ichiji-han
5. goji-han

No
When saying a telephone number, use *no* when stating where the dash belongs.

2. At a meeting in New York

ex. rokuji-han, gogo, yoru

> Sumisu: *Tōkyō-wa ima nanji desu-ka.*
> Tanaka: ***Rokuji-han** desu.*
> Sumisu: ***Gogo rokuji-han** desu-ka.*
> Tanaka: *Hai, sō desu. Tōkyō-wa ima
> **yoru** desu.*

1. goji, gozen, asa
2. hachiji-han, gogo, yoru
3. kuji, gogo, yoru
4. shichiji-han, gozen, asa
5. jūji, gogo, yoru

tokei
watch, clock

Tōkyō
Tokyo

-wa
denotes
subject

watashi
I, me

yoru
night

SELF-TEST

Translate the following sentences into Japanese:

1. Excuse me, what time is it?

2. The party is from 6:00 until 11:00.

3. Thank you very much.

4. My phone number is 251-9643.

5. Now it is 12:30 a.m.

6. What time is it in Tokyo?

7. It is morning in Tokyo.

8. It is evening in Tokyo.

9. Is it 3:00 p.m.?

10. That's right.

LESSON TWO
IKURA DESU-KA

In this lesson you will learn:

- How to ask for an object

- The days of the week

- The months of the year

- Multiples of one thousand

DIALOGUE

スミス: すみません。あの セーターは いくら ですか。
てんいん: どちらの セーター ですか。
スミス: あれ です。
てんいん: ああ。あの セーターは きゅうせん えん です。
スミス: そう ですか。この セーターも きゅうせん えん ですか。
てんいん: いいえ。その セーター は はっせん えん です。
スミス: これを ください。
てんいん: はい。ありがとう ございます。

Sumisu: *Sumimasen. Ano sētā-wa ikura desu-ka.*

Smith: Excuse me. How much is that sweater?

Ten'in: *Dochira-no sētā desu-ka.*

Clerk: Which sweater is it?

S: *Are desu.*

S: That one.

T: *Ā. Ano sētā-wa kyūsen en desu.*

C: Oh. That sweater is 9,000 yen.

S: *Sō desu-ka. Kono sētā-mo kyūsen en desu-ka.*

S: Really. Is this sweater also 9,000 yen?

T: *Iie. Sono sētā-wa hassen en desu.*

C: No. That sweater is 8,000 yen.

S: *Kore-o kudasai.*

S: I'd like this please.

T: *Hai. Arigatō gozaimasu.*

C: Yes. Thank you very much.

GRAMMAR EXPLANATION
1. Kore, kono

Kore refers to an object that is close to the speaker. It is usually followed by *wa*, *mo*, or *o* because it is always the subject or object of the sentence.

> ex. **Kore-wa** *pen desu.*
> This is a pen.
>
> **Kore-o** *kudasai.*
> I'll take this, please.

Kono has the same meaning as *kore*, but is always paired with a noun.

> ex. **Kono pen**-*wa yasui desu.*
> This pen is cheap.

2. Sore, sono

Sore and *sono* refer to objects that are close to the listener. They have the same grammar structure as *kore* and *kono*; *sore* is followed by *wa*, *mo*, or *o*, and *sono* is always paired with a noun.

> ex. **Sore-wa** *tokei desu.*
> It is a watch.
>
> **Sono tokei**-*wa ōkii desu.*
> That watch is big.

Prices
To state the price of an item, simply state the cost + *en*. *ex. jū en* (10 yen).

Yo
Yo is added at the end of a sentence when the speaker is telling the learner something that the learner probably did not know. *ex. Kore-wa nandesu-ka. Sore-wa tokei desu* **yo**. What is this? It's a clock (I'm informing you).

11

ano
that (with noun)

are
that

ashita
tomorrow

chigaimasu
is different, wrong

chiisai(i)
small

dochira
which one, choice of two

dono
which one(s), choice of three or more (with noun)

dore
which one(s), choice of three or more

en
yen

-ga
indicates subject or object

ikura
how much

kinō
yesterday

kono
this (with noun)

3. Are, ano

Are and *ano* are objects that are far from both the speaker and listener. They are used in the same grammatical patterns as *kore* and *kono*.

> *ex.* **Are-o** *kudasai.*
> I'll take that please.
>
> **Ano zubon**-wa ikura desu-ka.
> How much are those pants?

4. Dore, dono

Dore and *dono* mean "which one(s)" when there are three or more items to choose from. *Dore* is used as the subject or object of the sentence, and *dono* is always paired with a noun.

> *ex.* **Dore-ga** *anata-no desu-ka.*
> Which one is yours?
>
> **Dono wanpīsu**-ga anata-no desu-ka.
> Which dress is yours?

EXERCISES
1. Days of the week:

Sunday	*nichiyōbi*
Monday	*getsuyōbi*
Tuesday	*kayōbi*
Wednesday	*suiyōbi*

Thursday	*mokuyōbi*
Friday	*kinyōbi*
Saturday	*doyōbi*

The past form of **desu** is **deshita**.

2. Months in a year

The months are quite easy to learn. Simply state the number of each month (January = 1) and add *gatsu*:

Dore and *dono*+noun are usually followed by **ga** instead of *wa*.

January	*ichigatsu*
February	*nigatsu*
March	*sangatsu*
April	*shigatsu*
May	*gogatsu*
June	*rokugatsu*
July	*shichigatsu*
August	*hachigatsu*
September	*kugatsu*
October	*jūgatsu*
November	*jūichigatsu*
December	*jūnigatsu*

-O kudasai
-O kudasai is the phrase for letting someone know that you want to buy a certain object. *ex. Kono sētā-***o** *kudasai.* I would like this sweater.

3. Multiples of one thousand:

1,000 - *sen*	6,000 - *rokusen*
2,000 - *nisen*	7,000 - *nanasen*
3,000 - *sanzen*	8,000 - *hassen*
4,000 - *yonsen*	9,000 - *kyūsen*
5,000 - *gosen*	

kore
this

kyō
today

-mo
also, too, either

-o kudasai
I'll take ___ please

ōkii(i)
big

pen
pen

sō desu-ka
Really? Is that so?

sono
it (with noun)

sore
it

takai(i)
high, expensive

ten'in
sales clerk

yasui(i)
low, cheap

4. Look at the pictures below and ask for each item by saying "_____-o kudasai:"

SHORT DIALOGUES

1. Shopping

ex. zubon, hassen

Hayashi: Sono **zubon**-wa ikura desu-ka.
Ten'in: Kono **zubon**-wa **hassen** en desu.
Hayashi: Sore-o kudasai.
Ten'in: Hai, arigatō gozaimasu.

1. kutsushita, sen   4. wanpīsu, kyūsen
2. shatsu, gosen   5. sukāto, rokusen
3. bōshi, nisen

2. Two friends shopping together

> ex. kōto, kyūsen

> > Michiko: Kono **kōto**-wa **kyūsen** en desu.
> > Sumisu: Takai desu, ne.
> > Michiko: Iie, yasui desu, yo.
> > Sumisu: Sō desu-ka.
> > Michiko(to clerk): Kono **kōto**-o kudasai.

> > 1. kutsushita, sen
> > 2. shatsu, gosen
> > 3. bōshi, nisen
> > 4. wanpīsu, kyūsen
> > 5. sukāto, rokusen

3. ex. kinyōbi

> A: Kyō-wa nanyōbi desu-ka.
> B: Kyō-wa **kinyōbi** desu.

> > 1. nichiyōbi
> > 2. doyōbi
> > 3. suiyōbi
> > 4. getsuyōbi
> > 5. mokuyōbi

-mo
The article -mo can replace o, ga, or wa in a sentence.

Ne
Ne is often added to the end of sentences or phrases. It is similar in meaning to the Canadian eh.

CLOTHES

bōshi
hat

kōto
coat

kutsu
shoes

kutsushita
socks

nekutai
tie

sētā
sweater

shatsu
shirt

sukāto
skirt

wanpīsu
dress

zubon
pants

SELF-TEST

Translate the following sentences into Japanese:

1. Yesterday was Monday.

2. How much is that? (far from speaker and listener)

3. How much is that (far from speaker and listener) shirt?

4. This (close to speaker) dress is expensive.

5. Now, it is March.

Unscramble these sentences:

6. o kōto kudasai kono.

7. are desu wa ka ikura.

8. yasui desu ne sono wa nekutai.

9. ka nanyōbi wa kyō desu.

10. kudasai o bōshi sono.

LESSON THREE
DOKO-NI ARIMASU-KA

In this lesson you will learn:

- How to ask an object's location

- Prepositions

- Multiples of one hundred

DIALOGUE

I

たなか: スミスさん、こんにちは。

スミス: ああ。たなかさん、こんにちは。

たなか: あの くるまは スミスさんの ですか。

スミス: どの くるま ですか。

たなか: あの たてものの まえの くるま です。

スミス: いいえ。わたしの くるまは あの たてものの よこに
あります。

たなか: そう ですか。あの くるまは いい くるま ですね。

II

みちこ: くみこさん、わたしの かばんは どこに ありますか。

くみこ: テーブルの うえに ありませんか。

みちこ: はい、ありません。ああ、つくえの なかに ありますよ。

I	I
Tanaka: *Sumisu-san, konnichi-wa.*	Tanaka: Mr. Smith, good afternoon.
Sumisu: *Ā. Tanaka-san, konnichi-wa.*	Smith: Oh, Mr. Tanaka, good afternoon.
T: *Ano kuruma-wa Sumisu-san-no desu-ka.*	T: Is that your car, Mr. Smith?
S: *Dono kuruma desu-ka.*	S: Which car?
T: *Ano tatemono-no mae-no kuruma desu.*	T: The car in front of that building.

S: *Iie. Watashi-no kuruma-wa ano tatemono-no yoko-ni arimasu.*

T: *Sō desu-ka. Ano kuruma-wa ii kuruma desu, ne.*

II

Michiko: *Kumiko-san, watashi-no kaban-wa doko-ni arimasu-ka.*

Kumiko: *Tēburu-no ue-ni arimasen-ka.*

M: *Hai, arimasen. Ā, tsukue-no naka-ni arimasu yo.*

S: No. My car is beside that building.

T: Really. That car is very nice.

II

Michiko: Kumiko, where is my handbag?

Kumiko: Isn't it on the table?

M: Yes, it's not. Oh, it's in the desk.

Arimasu is used only when talking about non-living objects, and *imasu* is used for living things.

In Japanese, if a question is asked with a negative word, the answer is different than English. For example, "It isn't on the table?" in English is answered, "No, it's not." But in Japanese, *Hai, arimasen.* "Yes (that's right), it's not."

GRAMMAR EXPLANATION
1. The sentence structure for prepositions:

Subject-*wa* place-*no* preposition-*ni arimasu/ imasu.*

ex. *Pen-wa tēburu-no shita-ni arimasu.*
The pen is under the *table*.

Keitai bangō-wa tsukue-no ue-ni arimasu.
The cell phone number is on the desk.

ā
oh

arimasen
does not exist

arimasu
exist, have

doa
door

doko
where

enpitsu
pencil

hon
book

ii(i)
good

imasu
exist, to be

isu
chair

kaban
handbag

kami
paper

keitai (denwa)
cell phone

keitai bangō
cell phone number

kuruma
car

kyōdai
siblings

mado
window

mise
store, shop

ni
at, to

To state someone or something is in a general location, like a country, city, or building, use:

Subject-*wa* place-*ni arimasu/imasu.*

ex. *Tanaka-san-wa Tōkyō-ni imasu.*
Mrs. Tanaka is in Tokyo.

Nōto-wa ie-ni arimasu.
The notebook is in the house.

2. No

When *no* is added to the end of a noun, it shows possession. It is like the English " 's."

ex. *Kore-wa Michiko-san-no pen desu.*
This is Michiko's pen.

When describing where an object is, *no* is always added to the noun that shows where the object is.

ex. *Nōto-wa tēburu-no ue-ni arimasu.*
The notebook is on the table.

Kuruma-wa uchi-no ushiro-ni arimasu.
The car is behind the house.

3. Arimasu, imasu

Arimasu and *imasu* can be used to show that something exists, or that one has something.

ex. *Kono resutoran-ni-wa sushi-ga arimasu-ka?*
Does this restaurant have sushi?

*Anata-wa kyōdai-ga **imasu**-ka.*
Do you have any brothers or sisters?

EXERCISES
1. Looking at the pictures below, identify each item with a Japanese sentence:

ex.

➡ *Kore-wa **isu** desu.*

2. Answer the following questions:

*ex. **Hon**-wa doko-ni arimasu-ka.*
➡ ***Hon**-wa **tsukue**-no ue-ni arimasu.*

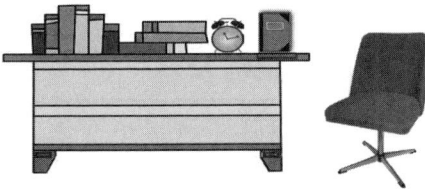

__Tokei__-wa doko-ni arimasu-ka.
__Isu__-wa doko-ni arimasu-ka.
__Nōto__-wa doko-ni arimasu-ka.

If the subject in the sentence is understood, it can be omitted.

Doko desu-ka
Doko desu-ka means "where is" something. However, *doko-ni arimasu-ka* means "*exactly* where is (something)," or "where is (something) *at*."

nōto
notebook

resutoran
restaurant

tatemono
building

tēburu
table

tsukue
desk

uchi
home

yoi
good

**PREPOSI-
TIONS**

aida
during, while,
between

mae
before, in
front of, ago

naka
in, inside

shita
down, under

soto
out, outside

ue
up, above

ushiro
behind, back

yoko
by, beside

3. Multiples of 100:

100 - *hyaku*	600 - *roppyaku*
200 - *nihyaku*	700 - *nanahyaku*
300 - *sanbyaku*	800 - *happyaku*
400 - *yonhyaku*	900 - *kyūhyaku*
500 - *gohyaku*	

SHORT DIALOGUES

1. *ex.* enpitsu, tsukue, naka

> Emiko: Michiko-san, **enpitsu**-wa doko-ni arimasu-ka.
> Michiko: **Enpitsu**-wa **tsukue**-no **naka**-ni arimasu.

1. pen, tēburu, ue
2. kami, tēburu, shita
3. kuruma, uchi, soto
4. nōto, isu, ue
5. anata-no zubon, tēburu, yoko
6. shatsu, doa, mae

22

2. *ex.* Naomi, uchi, naka

    A: ***Naomi**-san-wa doko-ni imasu-ka.*
    B: ***Naomi**-san-wa **uchi**-no **naka**-ni imasu.*

      1. Kaoru, doa, ushiro
      2. Jonson, uchi, soto
      3. Sumisu, kuruma, yoko
      4. Nobutaka, doa, mae
      5. Tokuichiro, kuruma, naka

ii
Both *yoi* and *ii* mean good; however, *ii* is generally used in conversation, while *yoi* is used primarily in writing.

3. *ex.* enpitsu, 50

    A: *Ano mise-ni-wa **enpitsu**-ga arimasu-ka.*
    B: *Hai, arimasu.*
    A: *Ikura desu-ka.*
    B: ***Gojū** en desu.*

      1. nōto, 100
      2. kami, 200
      3. pen, 150

COMMON EXPRESSIONS

ohayō gozaimasu
good morning

konnichi-wa
good afternoon

konban-wa
good evening

oyasumi nasai
good night

sayōnara
good bye

SELF-TEST

Fill in the missing particles with *wa, no, ni, san,* and *ka*:

1. Enpitsu ___ kaban ___ naka ___ arimasu.
2. Anata ___ hon ___ tēburu ___ ue ___ arimasu___.
3. Michiko ___ ___ kuruma ___ mae ___ imasu.
4. Emiko ___ ___ doko desu ___.
5. Isu ___ tēburu ___ ushiro ___ arimasu.

Unscramble the sentences:

6. naka no Jonson san arimasu wa nōto no ni tsukue.
7. arimasu doko watashi pen no wa ni ka.
8. wa kami tsukue shita no ni arimasu.
9. kutsu doko arimasu ni no ka Hara san wa.
10. Jonson san ni imasu resutoran wa.

LESSON FOUR
NANI-O SHIMASHITA-KA

In this lesson you will learn:

- Common verbs

- The past tense of verbs

- How to link two sentences

DIALOGUE

はら:	おはよう ございます。
スミス:	おはよう ございます。
はら:	きのう スミスさんは なにを しましたか。
スミス:	きのう にほんごを べんきょう しました。
はら:	そう ですか。テレビも みましたか。
スミス:	はい。テレビも みました。はらさんは なにを しましたか。
はら:	てがみを かきました。それ から ほんを よみました。ところで、きょうは どこに いきますか。
スミス:	おおさかに いきます。そして みちこさんに あいます。あなたは どこに いきますか。
はら:	とうきょうに いきます。そして とけいを かいます。
スミス:	それ では, さようなら。
はら:	さようなら。

Hara:	*Ohayō gozaimasu.*	Hara:	Good morning.
Sumisu:	*Ohayō gozaimasu.*	Smith:	Good morning.
H:	*Kinō, Sumisu-san-wa nani-o shimashita-ka.*	H:	Mr. Smith, what did you do yesterday?
S:	*Kinō Nihongo-o benkyō shimashita.*	S:	Yesterday I studied Japanese.
H:	*Sō desu-ka. Terebi-mo mimashita-ka.*	H:	Really. Did you also watch television?

S: *Hai. Terebi-mo mimashita. Hara-san-wa nani-o shimashita-ka.*

H: *Tegami-o kakimashita, sore kara hon-o yomimashita. Tokorode, kyō-wa doko-ni ikimasu-ka.*

S: *Ōsaka-ni ikimasu, soshite Michiko-san-ni aimasu. Anata-wa doko-ni ikimasu-ka.*

H: *Tōkyō-ni ikimasu, soshite tokei-o kaimasu.*

S: *Sore dewa, sayōnara.*

H: *Sayōnara.*

S: Yes, I also watched television. What did you do Mr. Hara?

H: I wrote a letter and then I read a book. By the way, where will you go today?

S: I will go to Osaka and I will meet Michiko. Where will you go today?

H: I will go to Tokyo and buy a watch.

S: Well, goodbye.

H: Goodbye.

O
Objects of sentences are always followed by o. *ex. Watashi-wa miruku-o nomimasu.* I drink milk. *Watashi-wa sushi-o tabemasu.* I eat sushi.

O-
O can be used as a prefix to many nouns to add honor or respect. *ex. sake, o-sake.*

GRAMMAR EXPLANATION
1. -Mashita

To change verbs to the past tense, simply change *masu* to *mashita.*

*ex. iki**masu***   go
    *iki**mashita***   went

    *hanashi**masu***   speak
    *hanashi**mashita***   spoke

Amerika America	
bideo video	

2. Ni

Ni always precedes *ikimasu, kimasu* and *kaerimasu* after a place is stated. In these instances, *ni* is used like the English "to." The grammar pattern is as follows:

ē yes (less formal than *hai*)

Eigo English

Subject-*wa* place-**ni** *ikimasu* (*kimasu* or *kaerimasu*)

ie house

ex. *Watashi-wa Hara-san-no ie-ni ikimasu.*
I go to Miss Hara's house.

īmēru e-mail

miruku milk

Harada-san-wa Amerika-ni kimashita.
Mr. Harada came to America.

mizu water

Mori-san-wa uchi-ni kaerimashita.
Mrs. Mori returned home.

Nihon Japan

Additionally, *ni* always precedes *aimasu.*

Nihongo Japanese language

ex. *Sumisu-san-ni aimashita.*
I met Mr. Smith.

rajio radio

Tanaka-san-wa Sumisu-san-ni aimashita-ka.
Did Mr. Tanaka meet Mr. Smith?

sake rice wine, alcohol

3. Soshite

sore dewa in that case

Soshite is a word that means "and." It is always used to link two sentences together.

sore kara then, after that

ex. *Watashi-wa Tōkyō-ni ikimasu.*
I go to Tokyo.

soshite and

tegami letter

Watashi-wa Nihongo-o benkyō shimasu.
I study Japanese.

*Watashi-wa Tōkyō-ni ikimasu **soshite**
Nihongo-o benkyō shimasu.*

I go to Tokyo **and** study Japanese.

*Hara-san-wa īmēru-o yomimasu **soshite**
bideo-o mimasu.*

Miss Hara reads e-mail **and** watches a video.

EXERCISES
1. Verbs

Identify each verb in the pictures below:

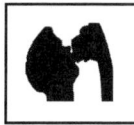

There is no distinction between present tense verbs and future tense in Japanese. Whether or not the action takes place currently or in the future depends on the context of the sentence.

terebi
television

tokorode
by the way

VERBS

aimasu
meet

arukimasu
walk

benkyō shimasu
study

hanashimasu
speak

hashirimasu
run

ikimasu
go

kaerimasu
return (go back)

kaimasu
buy

kakimasu
write

kikimasu
listen

kimasu
come

mimasu
see

nemasu
sleep

nomimasu
drink

2. Past tense

Change the following verbs into past tense by placing them into the following sentence:

ex. imasu
➡ *Hara-san-wa **imashita**.*
  arukimasu   hashirimasu
  wakarimasu   nemasu

ex. Nihongo, benkyō shimasu
➡ *Watashi-wa **Nihongo**-o **benkyō shimashita**.*
  mizu, nomimasu
  rajio, kikimasu
  terebi, mimasu
  kuruma, unten shimasu
  kutsushita, kaimasu
  Eigo, oshiemasu
  sushi, tabemasu
  bideo, mimasu
  īmēru, yomimasu

ex. Kyōto, ikimasu
  A: *Anata-wa **Kyōto**-ni **ikimashita**-ka.*
  B: *Ē, **Kyōto**-ni **ikimashita**.*
  Nihon, kimasu
  ie, kaerimasu
  Yamada-san, aimasu
  Amerika, ikimasu

30

SHORT DIALOGUES
1. Two friends talking

ex. nichiyōbi, benkyō shimashita

Tanaka: Jonson-san-wa **nichiyōbi**
nani-o shimashita-ka.
Jonson: **Nichiyōbi** *watashi-wa* **benkyō**
shimashita.

1. mokuyōbi, Michiko-san-ni aimashita
2. getsuyōbi, Tōkyō-ni ikimashita
3. suiyōbi, Nihon-ni kimashita
4. kinō, hon-o yomimashita

2. Two friends talking

ex. hon-o yomimashita

Tanaka: Sumisu-san, kinō-wa **hon-o**
yomimashita-*ka.*
Sumisu: Hai, **hon-o yomimashita**.
Tanaka: Nihongo-mo benkyō
shimashita-ka.
Sumisu: Hai, Nihongo-mo benkyō
shimashita.

1. o-sake-o nomimashita
2. terebi-o mimashita
3. rajio-o kikimashita
4. eigo-o oshiemashita

Oshiemasu
Oshiemasu means "teach," but it also means "tell." If you want a person to tell you information about something, use *oshiemasu.*

Aimasu
Aimasu is used not only when you meet someone for the first time, but also whenever you see someone. For example, one would say "I saw Kate at the mall," in English, but in Japanese, one would use *aimasu* (meet) instead of *mimasu* (see).

31

**VERBS
(cont.)**

oshiemasu
teach

shimasu
do

tabemasu
eat

*unten
shimasu*
drive

wakarimasu
understand

yomimasu
read

3. *ex.* Tōkyō, jūichiji

    Yuki: Doko-ni ikimashita-ka.
    Hiroko: **Tōkyō**-*ni ikimashita.*
    Yuki: Nanji-ni kaerimashita-ka.
    Hiroko: **Jūichiji** *ni kaerimashita.*

    1. Ōsaka, jūniji
    2. Yokohama, jūichiji
    3. Kyōto, niji

SELF-TEST

Fill in the missing particles with *wa, no, ni, san, o,* and *ka*:

1. Jonson ___ ___ sushi ___ tabemashita.

2. Watashi ___ mizu ___ nomimashita.

3. Michiko ___ ___ Tōkyō ___ kimashita.

4. Watashi ___ Nihongo ___ benkyō shimasu.

5. Kinō, Jonson ___ ___ terebi ___ mimashita ___.

Translate the following sentences into Japanese:

6. Today, I teach English.

7. Yesterday, Michiko came to America.

8. Does Mrs. Smith run?

9. I read (past) a book.

10. I speak Japanese.

LESSON FIVE
NIHONGO-O HANASHIMASEN

In this lesson you will learn:

- Family terms

- The negative form of verbs

- The plain form of verbs

DIALOGUE

I

A:　　　スミスさん、こちらは たなかさん です。

たなか: はじめまして たなか です。

スミス: はじめまして スミス です。どうぞ よろしく

たなか: にほんに どの くらい いますか。

スミス: ごかげつ です。その あいだに、えいごを おしえて
いました。

たなか: かぞくも きましたか。

スミス: おとうとは きました。

たなか: おとうとさんは にほんごを はなしますか。

スミス: いいえ。おとうとは にほんごを はなしません。

II

A: あの おんなのひとは だれ ですか。

B: その おんなのひとは どこに いますか。

A: くるまの そとに います。

B: ああ。かのじょは やましたさんの おくさん です。

I

A: *Sumisu-san, kochira-wa Tanaka-san desu.*

T: *Hajimemashite, Tanaka desu.*

I

A: Mr. Smith, this is Mr. Tanaka.

T: How do you do, I'm Mr. Tanaka.

S: *Hajimemashite, Sumisu desu. Dōzo, yoroshiku.*

S: How do you do, I'm Mr. Smith. Pleased to meet you.

T: *Nihon-ni dono kurai imasu-ka.*

T: How long have you been in Japan?

S: *Gokagetsu desu. Sono aida-ni, Eigo-o oshiete imashita.*

S: Five months. During that time, I have been teaching English.

T: *Kazoku-mo kimashita-ka.*

T: Did your family also come?

S: *Otōto-wa kimashita.*

S: My younger brother came.

T: *Otōto-san-wa Nihongo-o hanashimasu-ka.*

T: Does your brother speak Japanese?

S: *Iie. Otōto-wa Nihongo-o hanashimasen.*

S: No, he does not speak Japanese.

II

II

A: *Ano onnanohito-wa dare desu-ka.*

A: Who is that woman over there?

B: *Sono onnanohito-wa doko-ni imasu-ka.*

B: Where is the woman?

A: *Kuruma-no soto-ni imasu.*

A: Outside of the car.

B: *Ā. Kanojo-wa Yamashita-san-no oku-san desu.*

B: Oh. She is Mr. Yamashita's wife.

Sensei
Sensei is a term that means "teacher," but is not solely used when referring to a teacher. Any person who is in a position of high authority or respect can be addressed as *sensei*.

Mada
When *mada* is used to mean "yet" it is always paired with a negative verb. *Sumisu-san-wa **mada** kimasen.* Mr. Smith did not come yet.

35

dare
who

dono
(g)kurai
how long

dōzo
yoroshiku
I'm pleased to
meet you (lit.
- please be
good to me)

gakusei
student

gokagetsu
five months

hajime-
mashite
how do you
do (lit. - for
the first time)

hito
person

kanojo
she

kare
he

kata
person
(polite)

kochira
this way,
polite for *kore*

kodomo
child

kodomotachi
children

GRAMMAR EXPLANATION
1. Negative verbs

To change verbs to a negative, change the *su* at
the end of the verb to *sen*.

ex. *ikima**su***   go
     *ikima**sen***   don't go

     *unten shima**su***   drive
     *unten shima**sen***   don't drive

The negative form of *desu* is *dewa arimasen*.

*Sensei **dewa arimasen**.*
Is not a teacher.

*Gakusei **dewa arimasen**.*
Is not a student.

2. Asking Names

To ask someone their name, say:
   Anata-no namae-wa nandesu-ka.
To answer:
   Watashi-no namae-wa _____ desu.

ex. *Anata-no namae-wa nandesu-ka.*
   *Watashi-no namae-wa **Hiroko** desu.*

This question is usually asked by a person of
higher position to their subordinate, like a teacher
asking a student.

36

EXERCISES

1. Look at the pictures below and state each person's family role (some have more than one). Also identify man, woman, girl, boy and baby:

2. Change the following verbs to negatives:

ex. arukimasu

➡ *arukimasen*

aimasu	unten shimasu
imasu	yomimasu
hanashimasu	tabemasu
ikimasu	wakarimasu
kaerimasu	shimasu
kakimasu	oshiemasu
kikimasu	hashirimasu
nemasu	nomimasu
benkyō shimasu	

Onnano
Onnano means "female," *hito* means "person," *ko* is "child." Therefore, *onnano+hito* means "woman," and *onnano+ko* means "girl."

Otokono
Otokono means "male;" therefore, *otokono+hito* means "man," and *otokono+ko* means "boy."

mada (not) yet, still	**3. The plain form of the verbs is as follows:**

namae
name

onnanohito
woman

onnanoko
girl

oshiete imashita
have been teaching

Ōsutoraria
Australia

otokonohito
man

otokonoko
boy

sensei
teacher

tomodachi
friend

aimasu	*au(-u)*
arimasu	*aru(-u)*
arukimasu	*aruku(-u)*
benkyō shimasu	*benkyō suru*
chigaimasu	*chigau(-u)*
desu	*da*
hanashimasu	*hanasu(-u)*
hashirimasu	*hashiru(-ru)*
ikimasu	*iku(-u)*
imasu	*iru(-ru)*
kaerimasu	*kaeru(-u)*
kaimasu	*kau(-u)*
kakimasu	*kaku(-u)*
kikimasu	*kiku(-u)*
kimasu	*kuru(irregular)*
mimasu	*miru(-ru)*
nemasu	*neru(-u)*
nomimasu	*nomu(-u)*
oshiemasu	*oshieru(-ru)*
shimasu	*suru(irregular)*
tabemasu	*taberu(-ru)*
unten shimasu	*unten suru*
wakarimasu	*wakaru(-u)*
yomimasu	*yomu(-u)*

From this point forward, verbs will be introduced in their plain form.

38

To conjugate the plain form into the -*masu* form:

For -*u* verbs, drop the final *u* and add *imasu*

*ex. a**u***	*a**imasu***
*nom**u***	*nomi**masu***

The *si* sound does not exist in Japanese, only *shi*. When -*u* verbs end in *su*, *shimasu* must be used.

*ex. hana**su***	*hana**shimasu***

For -*ru* verbs, if the letter preceding the final *ru* is an *i* or *e*, drop *ru* and add *masu*

*ex. mi**ru***	*mi**masu***
*oshie**ru***	*oshie**masu***

If the letter preceding the final *ru* is an *a* or *o*, drop *ru* and add *rimasu*

*ex. a**ru***	*a**rimasu***

SHORT DIALOGUES

1. At school

ex. Megumi

Sensei: Anata-no namae-wa nandesu-ka.
Gakusei: Watashi-no namae-wa **_Megumi_** desu.

1. Takeshi   2. Keigo
3. Masāki   4. Nobutaka
5. Tokuichiro

Dare
If *dare* is the subject and the person is unknown, use *ga* after *dare*, if the person is known, use *wa*.

Pronouns
The personal pronouns *kanojo* and *kare* are not used in Japanese as frequently as the English she and he, as they are considered informal words. First or last names + *san* are used more often.

FAMILY TERMS

okā-san
mother

otō-san
father

oku-san
wife

go-shujin
husband

onē-san
older sister

imōto-san
younger sister

onii-san
older brother

otōto-san
younger brother

obā-san
grandmother
(old woman)

oba-san
aunt

ojii-san
grandfather
(old man)

oji-san
uncle

kazoku
family

akachan
baby

2. At a party

ex. Jonson, Tanaka, Amerika

Introducer: **Jonson**-san, kochira-wa
Tanaka-san desu.

A: Hajimemashite, **Tanaka** desu.
B: Hajimemashite, **Jonson** desu.
Dōzo yoroshiku.
A: **Jonson**-san-wa **Amerika**-no kata
desu-ka.
A: Hai, **Amerika** kara kimashita.

1. Jonson, Hirakawa, Amerika
2. Sumisu, Nishiyama, Ōsutoraria
3. Aoki, Tanaka, Tōkyō
4. Hanabusa, Tanaka, Tōkyō
5. Tanaka, Mōri, Kyōto

3. At school

ex. Eigo-o, benkyō suru

A: Kyō, anata-wa **Eigo-o**
benkyō shimasu-ka.
B: Iie, **benkyō shimasen**.
A: Nani-o shimasu-ka.
B: Mada wakarimasen.

1. Kyōto-ni, iku
2. bideo-o, miru
3. o-sake-o, nomu
4. hon-o, yomu

SELF TEST

Translate the following into Japanese:

1. This is Michiko's grandmother.

2. How do you do?

3. Nice to meet you.

4. What is your name?

5. Today his father does not study English.

Unscramble the following sentences:

6. wa o no imōto san Mitsumura san tabemasen sushi.

7. yomimashita onii san Tanaka san hon no kinō o wa.

8. no namae Jonson desu watashi wa.

9. no no no ni wa oba san naka arimasen anata hon tsukue.

10. watashi wa ni aimashita tomodachi kinō.

LESSON SIX
IKIMASHŌ

In this lesson you will learn:

- Colors

- The -mashō form of verbs

- The past negative form of verbs

DIALOGUE

I

A: きのう おともだちに あいましたか。

B: いいえ、あいません でした。

A: なにを しましたか。

B: えいがかんに いきました 。アクション えいが を みました。
えいごは よく わかりません でした, でも とても いい えいが
でした。あなたは なにを しましたか。

A: わたしは マクドナルドに いきました。それ から, デパートに
いきました。

B: そう ですか。なにを かいましたか。

A: きいろい セ―タ―を かいました。

B: ずぼんも かいましたか。

A: いいえ、かいません でした。

II

A: これ から どこに いきましょうか。

B: そう ですね。いせたん デパートに いきましょうか。バ―ゲンが
あります。

A: それは いい ですね。そこに いきましょう。

I	I
A: *Kinō o-tomodachi-ni aimashita-ka.*	A: Yesterday, did you meet your friend?
B: *Iie, aimasen deshita.*	B: No, I didn't.
A: *Nani-o shimashita-ka.*	A: What did you do?
B: *Eigakan-ni ikimashita. Akushon eiga-o mimashita. Eigo-wa*	B: I went to the movie theater. I saw an action film. I didn't understand

yoku wakarimasen deshita, demo totemo ii eiga deshita. Anata-wa nani-o shimashita-ka.

the English very well, but it was a very good movie. What did you do?

A: *Watashi-wa Makudonarudo-ni ikimashita. Sore kara, depāto-ni ikimashita.*

A: I went to McDonald's. Then, I went to a department store.

B: *Sō desu-ka. Nani-o kaimashita-ka.*

B: Really. What did you buy?

A: *Kiiroi sētā-o kaimashita.*

A: I bought a yellow sweater.

B: *Zubon-mo kaimashita-ka.*

B: Did you buy pants too?

A: *Iie. Kaimasen deshita.*

A: No, I didn't.

II

II

A: *Kore-kara doko-ni ikimashō-ka.*

A: Where shall we go from here?

B: *Sō desu-ne. Isetan depāto-ni ikimashō-ka. Bāgen-ga arimasu.*

B: Well, should we go to Isetan? They are having a sale.

A: *Sore-wa ii desu, ne. Soko-ni ikimashō.*

A: That's great. Let's go there.

As you will note in the dialogue, many of the places named are non-Japanese words changed to fit into their phoneitic system. For instance, "McDonald's" becomes *Makudonarudo*. "Seven-Eleven" becomes *Sebun Irebun*. Speaking of Seven-Eleven, some find these stores a little more upscale in Asia than in western countries. They are a great place for authentic local snacks.

-Jin
To say a person is Japanese, Australian, etc., add *-jin* to the country's name. ex. *Nihonjin* = Japanese person, *Ōsutorariajin* = Australian.

45

asoko
over there

bāgen
bargain (sale)

bīru
beer

demo
but

eiga
movie

gohan
rice, meal

Isetan
a department
store in Japan

koko
here

kōhī
coffee

ocha
tea

shinbun
newspaper

soko
there

totemo
very

yoku
well

GRAMMAR EXPLANATION

1. Colors

Only six colors can stand alone as adjectives: *akai, aoi, chairoi, kiiroi, kuroi,* and *shiroi.*

ex. *Kuruma-wa **akai** desu.*　　***akai** kuruma*
The car is red.　　　　　　red car

*Hon-wa **kuroi** desu.*　　***kuroi** hon*
The book is black.　　　　black book

To use these color words as nouns, drop the final *i*:

ex. ***Aka**-wa ii iro desu.*
Red is a nice color.

Other color adjectives cannot stand alone. When these colors are used as predicate adjectives, state the color + *iro.*

ex. *Kuruma-wa **orenji iro** desu.*
The car is orange.

*Hon-wa **midori iro** desu.*
The book is green.

When these colors directly modify nouns, state the color + *iro-no.*

ex. ***orenji iro-no** kuruma*
orange car

***midori iro-no** hon*
green book

To use these colors as nouns, use the color + *iro:*

*ex. **Murasaki iro**-wa ii iro desu.*
Purple is a nice color.

2. -Mashō

To change a verb to mean let's+verb, change the *masu* to *mashō*.

*ex. iki**masu***
*iki**mashō*** Let's go.

*nomi**masu***
*nomi**mashō*** Let's drink.

3. Verbs, Past Negative Tense

To change a verb to past negative tense (did not + verb), change the *masu* to *masen* and add *deshita*.

*ex. iki**masu***
*iki**masen deshita*** did not go

*nomi**masu***
*nomi**masen deshita*** did not drink

*Watashi-wa yakkyoku-ni iki**masu**.*
I go to the pharmacy.

*Watashi-wa yakkyoku-ni iki**masen deshita**.*
I didn't go to the pharmacy.

*Kare-wa kōhī-o nomi**masen**.*
He doesn't drink coffee.

*Kare-wa kōhī-o nomi**masen deshita**.*
He didn't drink coffee.

*biyōin dewa ari**masen deshita***
was not a beauty shop

PLACES

apāto
apartment

biyōin
beauty shop

byōin
hospital

depāto
department
store

eigakan
movie theater

eki
station

gakkō
school

ginkō
bank

hoteru
hotel

**sūpāmā-
ketto**
supermarket

yakkyoku,
kusuriya
pharmacy

yūbinkyoku
post office

EXERCISES
1. -Mashō

Change the following verbs into the *mashō* form:

ex. arukimasu
➡ *arukimashō*

aimasu   nemasu
tabemasu   shimasu
ikimasu   hanashimasu
benkyō shimasu

2. Past negative

Substitute the given words into the following sentences:

ex. arukimasu
A: *Hanabusa-san-wa* **arukimashita**-*ka.*
B: *Iie, Hanabusa-san-wa* **arukimasen
deshita**.

Kaerimasu   unten shimasu
kakimasu   wakarimasu
kikimasu   yomimasu
mimasu   nomimasu

SHORT DIALOGUES
1. *ex.* hon, yomu

> *Masāki: Keigo-san, nani-o shimashō-ka.*
> *Keigo:* **Hon**-o **yomimashō**.

   1. gohan, taberu
   2. terebi, miru
   3. Nihongo, benkyō suru
   4. o-sake, nomu

2. *ex.* eigakan

> *Megumi: Takeshi-san, doko-ni ikimashō-ka.*
> *Takeshi:* **Eigakan**-ni ikimashō.

   1. yūbinkyoku
   2. ginkō
   3. depāto
   4. sūpāmāketto
   5. Tōkyō

3. *ex.* terebi, miru, bideo

> A: *Kinō, nani-o shimashita-ka.*
> B: **Terebi**-o **mimashita**.
> A: **Bideo**-mo **mimashita**-ka.
> B: *Iie, nani-mo **mimasen** deshita.*

   1. hon, yomu, shinbun
   2. bīru, nomu, o-sake
   3. eiga, miru, terebi
   4. shatsu, kau, kutsu

Sō desu ne
This expression can also mean "let me see . . ." It is sometimes used as a refusal. Often times, Japanese people consider it impolite to say "no" in a straightforward manner. Be sensitive to a person who uses this phrase. They may need time to think over what has been said, or may be politely trying to tell you "no."

Many Japanese department stores have amazing food markets and bakeries in the basement level.

COLORS

aka(i)
red

ao(i)
blue

chairo(i)
brown

iro
color

kiiro(i)
yellow

kuro(i)
black

midori (iro)
green

murasaki (iro)
purple

orenji (iro)
orange

shiro(i)
white

4. *ex.* midori

A: *Jonson-san-no kuruma-wa nani iro desu-ka.*
B: *Jonson-san-no kuruma-wa **midori iro** desu.*
A: *Anata-no ie-ni-mo **midori iro-no** kuruma-ga arimasu-ka.*
B: *Hai, arimasu.*

1. aka
2. chairo
3. kiiro
4. ao
5. kuro
6. orenji

SELF-TEST
Translate the following sentences into Japanese:

1. Let's sleep.

2. Let's go to the movie theater.

3. I didn't go to the hospital.

4. Didn't you drink tea?

5. I didn't drive a blue car.

6. I see a purple desk.

7. Did you go to the beauty salon?

8. That woman reads a red book.

9. That (far from speaker and listener) white building is a bank.

10. He is in the restaurant.

LESSON SEVEN
KANTAN DESU

In this lesson you will learn:

- Common adjectives
- Successive adjectives
- Expressing likes and dislikes

DIALOGUE

I

A: きょうは レストランに いきましょうか。

B: どこの レストランに いきましょうか。

A: レッド ロブスターは どう ですか。

B: そう ですね。ほかの レストランは どう ですか。

A: それ では にほん しょくの レストランに いきましょう。

B: はい。

A: この レストランの しょくじは おいしい ですか。

B: はい。ここは おいしくて やすい です。

A: ここには おはしが ありますか。

B: はい、あります。

A: むずかしい ですか。

B: いいえ。かんたん です。

II

A: きれいな セーター ですね。あたらしいの ですか。

B: はい。きのう かいました。

A: どこで かいましたか。

B: いせたんで かいました。

I	I
A: *Kyō-wa resutoran-ni ikimashō-ka.*	A: Shall we go to a restaurant today?
B: *Doko-no resutoran-ni ikimashō-ka.*	B: Where (restaurant) shall we go?
A: *Reddo Robusutā-wa dō desu-ka.*	A: How about Red Lobster?

B: *Sō desu ne. Hoka-no resutoran-wa dō desu-ka.*

A: *Sore dewa Nihon shoku-no resutoran-ni ikimashō.*

B: *Hai.*

A: *Kono resutoran-no shokuji-wa oishii desu-ka.*

B: *Hai. Koko-wa oishi-kute yasui desu.*

A: *Koko-ni-wa o-hashi-ga arimasu-ka.*

B: *Hai, arimasu.*

A: *Muzukashii desu-ka.*

B: *Iie. Kantan desu.*

II

A: *Kireina sētā desu, ne. Atarashii-no desu-ka.*

B: *Hai. Kinō kaimashita.*

A: *Doko-de kaimashita-ka.*

B: *Isetan-de kaimashita.*

B: Well... what about another restaurant?

A: In that case, let's go to a Japanese restaurant.

B: O.K.

A: Is the food in this restaurant good?

B: Yes. It's good and reasonably priced.

A: Do they use chop sticks here?

B: Yes, they do.

A: Are they difficult?

B: No. They are simple.

II

A: That is a pretty sweater. Is it a new one?

B: Yes. I bought it yesterday.

A: Where did you buy it?

B: I bought it at Isetan.

Fast Food
Many Western fast food chains have establishments in Japan, like McDonald's, Kentucky Fried Chicken, Taco Bell and Pizza Hut. Usually the names of the food items are the same as they are in English, but they are written in *Katakana* and pronounced within the Japanese phonetic system. Some examples are *hanbāgā* (hamburger), *pepushi* (Pepsi), *koka kōra* (Coca-Cola), *furaido poteto* (french fries).

53

akarui(i)
bright

amari
(not) much

atarashii(i)
new

atsui(i)
hot

daisuki(na)
like very
much

-de
indicates
an action's
location

dō
what way,
how about

(o)hashi
chopsticks

hayai(i)
fast, early

hiroi(i)
spacious

hoka-no
other

kantan(na)
simple

karai(i)
spicy hot

kirai(na)
dislike, hate

kirei(na)
beautiful

GRAMMAR EXPLANATION
1. I and Na Adjectives

i **adjectives**: The final *i* is used when stating an adjective in the present tense, regardless of its position in the sentence.

ex. oishii
oishii tenpura
delicious tempura
Tenpura-wa oishii desu.
The tempura was delicious.

na **adjectives**: When a *na* adjective is used directly before a noun, use *na*. However, when it stands alone, do not say *na*.

ex. kirei
kireina sētā
beautiful sweater
Sētā-wa kirei desu.
The sweater is beautiful.

2. Two Successive Adjectives

In English, when using two adjectives, the word "and" usually connects them. However, in Japanese, the word *to* is not used. *To* usually connects nouns only.

When stating successive adjectives, if the first adjective is an *i* adjective, drop the final *i* and add *kute.*

ex. Kuruma-wa akakute ōkii desu.
The car is red and big.

*Nihon-no ie-wa **chiisakute takai** desu.*
Japanese houses are small and expensive.

If the first adjective is a *na* adjective, simply add *de* to the end of it.

> *ex. Amerika-wa **kirei-de hiroi** desu.*
> America is beautiful and spacious.

3. Suki desu, Kirai desu

When stating that you like or dislike something, the following sentence pattern is always used:

> _____*-ga suki desu.*   _____*-ga kirai desu.*

> *ex. Bīru-**ga suki desu**.*
> I like beer.

> *Karei-**ga kirai desu**.*
> I strongly dislike curry.

4. -De

When stating a location where an action was performed, the article *de* always follows the place's name. It is similar to the English "at."

> *ex. Gakkō-**de** Nihongo-o benkyō shimashita.*
> At school, I studied Japanese.

> *Eigakan-**de**, Michiko-san-ni aimasen deshita.*
> At the theater, I did not meet (see) Michiko.

Amari
Amari is always paired with a negative verb and usually comes directly before a verb.
*ex. Watashi-wa Nihongo-o **amari** benkyō shimasen deshita.* I did not study Japanese very much.

Dō
Dō is in another set of *kosoado* word.
Kō (this way), *sō* (that way) and *ā* (that way) are the others.

kurai(i)
dark

muzukashii(i)
difficult

oishii(i)
delicious

omoshiroi(i)
interesting,
fun

osoi(i)
slow, late

samui(i)
cold

shoku
meal, diet

shokuji
a meal, dinner

suki(na)
likeable

to
and, with

tokoro
place

yasashii(i)
easy

EXERCISES
1. Adjectives

Combine the following adjectives:

ex. ōkii, takai desu
➡ *ōkikute takai desu*

    chiisai, yasui desu
    kirei, omoshiroi desu
    hayai, chiisai desu
    osoi, shiroi desu
    akai, atsui desu
    akarui, ōkii desu
    kantan, omoshiroi desu

2. Suki desu, kirai desu

Use the following words in either of these
sentences:

_____-ga suki desu.   _____-ga kirai desu.

sushi	*akai kuruma*
byōin	*oishii tabemono*
miruku	*Nihongo*
pan	*kono hon*
ringo	*murasaki iro-no zubon*

3. -De

Match the following phrases:

1. *gakkō-de*	a. *terebi-o mimashita*
2. *eigakan-de*	b. *benkyō shimashita*
3. *resutoran-de*	c. *nemashita*
4. *uchi-de*	d. *eiga-o mimashita*
5. *hoteru-de*	e. *gohan-o tabemashita*

SHORT DIALOGUES

1. *ex.* sushi, oishii

   A: *Kono resutoran-ni-wa **sushi**-ga arimasu-ka.*
   B: *Hai, sushi-ga arimasu.*
   A: ***Oishii** desu-ka.*
   B: *Hai, totemo **oishii** desu.*

   1. akai budōshu, takai
   2. karei, karai
   3. o-sashimi, oishii

2. *ex.* Toyota-no kuruma, Matsuda-no kuruma

   A: *Sumisu-san-wa **Toyota-no kuruma**-ga suki desu-ka.*
   B: *Hai, daisuki desu.*
   A: ***Matsuda-no kuruma**-mo suki desu-ka.*
   B: *Iie, amari suki dewa arimasen.*

   1. atsui sake, bīru
   2. hayai kuruma, ōkii kuruma
   3. Nihon, Nihon-no shokuji
   4. Nihongo, kanji
   5. o-sakana, o-sashimi

If you do not like a particular food and do not wish to offend the person you are with, do not use the word *kirai* because it is too strong. Instead, you should say *amari suki dewa arimasen*, which means "I do not really care for it," or "I don't like it very much."

Ya
Ya is often added to the end of a word to charge that word into a store name.
ex. kusuri = medicine, *kusuri**ya*** = pharmacy; *sakana* = fish, *sakana**ya*** = fish store; *niku* = meat, *niku**ya*** = meat store; *hon* = book, *hon**ya*** = book store.

FOOD

budōshu
wine

jūsu
juice

(o)kashi
snack

karei
curry

niku
meat

pan
bread

ringo
apple

(o)sakana
fish

(o)sashimi
raw fish dish

sukiyaki
meat dish

tabemono
food

tenpura
fried
shrimp and
vegetables

wasabi
very hot
mustard

3. *ex.* ōkii, kirei, o-sake-o nomu

A: *Tanaka-san-no ie-wa **ōkikute kirei** desu, ne.*
B: *Iie, uchi-wa chiisai desu.*
A: *Koko-de **o-sake-o nomimashō**-ka.*
B: *Hai sō shimashō.*

1. kirei, hiroi, gohan-o taberu
2. hiroi, kirei, ocha-o nomu
3. kirei, ōkii, bideo-o mini

SELF-TEST

Fill in the missing blanks with *san, wa, ga, de, o, kute, no, ni,* or *ka*:

1. Kuruma _____ kiiro _____ chiisai desu.

2. Akai budōshu _____ arimasu _____.

3. Asoko _____ gohan _____ tabemashita.

4. Tanaka _____ _____ ie _____ yasashii hon _____ yomimashita.

5. Sumisu _____ _____ _____ -sashimi _____ suki desu _____.

Translate the following sentences into Japanese:

6. It is beautiful and expensive.

7. Is karashi delicious?

8. I don't really care for white wine.

9. At school, I didn't study Japanese.

10. I like Tokyo very much.

LESSON EIGHT
NANI-O SHITE IMASU-KA

In this lesson you will learn:

- The -te imasu verb form
- Common verbs

DIALOGUE

I

A: いま ひらかわさんと でんわで はなしました。

B: そう ですか。それで ひらかわさんは なにを して いますか。

A: ひらかわさんは いま ごはんを つくって います。

B: ひらかわさんは おげんき ですか。

A: はい、げんき です。

B: ちょっと まって ください。いま おちゃを いれて います から。

A: どうぞ おかまいなく。

II

はら: もりたさん こんにちは。

もりた: こんにちは。あなたの ごかぞくは いかが ですか。
いそがしい ですか。

はら: とても いそがしい です。しゅじんは ふじ ぎんこうに
つとめて います。むすめは じゅくで べんきょう して
います。むすこは サッカーを して います。そして わたしは
いろいろな ことを して います。

もりた: そう ですか。それは たいへん ですね。

I

A: *Ima Hirakawa-
san-to denwa-de
hanashimashita.*

B: *Sō desu-ka. Sorede
Hirakawa-san-wa
nani-o shite imasu-ka.*

I

A: I just talked with Mrs.
Hirakawa on the
phone.

B: Really. What is Mrs.
Hirakawa doing?

A: *Hirakawa-san-wa ima gohan-o tsukutte imasu.*

B: *Hirakawa-san-wa o-genki desu-ka.*

A: *Hai, genki desu.*

B: *Chotto matte kudasai. Ima ocha-o irete imasu kara.*

A: *Dōzo okamainaku.*

II

Hara: *Morita-san, konnichi-wa.*

Morita: *Konnichi-wa. Anata-no go-kazoku-wa ikaga desu-ka. Isogashii desu-ka.*

H: *Totemo isogashii desu. Shujin-wa Fuji ginkō-ni tsutomete imasu. Musume-wa juku-de benkyō shite imasu. Musuko-wa sakkā-o shite imasu. Soshite watashi-wa iroirona koto-o shite imasu.*

M: *Sō desu-ka. Sore-wa taihen desu ne.*

A: Now Mrs. Hirakawa is making a meal.

B: Is Mrs. Hirakawa healthy?

A: Yes, she's healthy.

B: Just a moment please. I'm pouring some tea.

A: Please don't trouble yourself.

II

Hara: Mrs. Morita, good afternoon.

Morita: Good afternoon. How is your family? Are they busy?

H: Very busy. My husband is working at Fuji Bank. My daughter is studying at *juku*. My son is playing soccer, and I'm doing a variety of things.

M: Really. That's tough, isn't it.

Chotto matte kudasai
This phrase means "please wait a moment."

Dōzo
Dōzo can take on a wide variety of meanings, depending on how it is used. Generally speaking, it means "please accept this," or "please go ahead." Japanese people frequently say *dōzo* when presenting a gift, telling someone to go ahead and eat or drink, or when inviting someone into their home.

VERBS

ageru(-ru)
to give

asobu(-u)
to play

dekakeru(-ru)
to leave, go
out

dekiru(-ru)
can do, is
possible to do

*denwa-o
kakeru*
to talk on the
phone

furu(-u)
to fall (rain or
snow)

hairu(-u)
to enter

ireru(-u)
to put in, to
pour

iu(-u)
to say

matsu(-u)
to wait

narau(-u)
to learn

naru(-u)
to become

noru(-u)
to ride

okiru(-ru)
to awake,
wake up

GRAMMAR EXPLANATION

1. -Te imasu

This verb tense is the same as the English progressive form, verb+ing.

> *ex. Watashi-wa **matte imasu**.*
> I am waiting.
>
> *Ame-ga **futte imasu**.*
> It is raining.
>
> *Tanaka-san-wa **benkyō shite imasu**.*
> Mr. Tanaka is studying.

Shite imasu also describes something that one has been doing in the past, and continues to do now, like the English "I have been _____ ing."

> *ex. Ichinenkan Nihongo-o **benkyō shite imasu**.*
> I have been studying Japanese for one year.
>
> *Hirakawa-san-wa Amerika-ni **sunde imasu**.*
> Mr. Hirakawa has been living in America.

2. Conjugating verbs into present continuous

For *-u* verbs change:

bu	→	*-nde*	*asobu*	*aso**nde***
gu	→	*-ide*	*isogu*	*iso**ide*** (L. 12)
ku	→	*-ite*	*kiku*	*ki**ite***
mu, nu	→	*-nde*	*nomu*	*no**nde***
ru	→	*-tte*	*hashiru*	*hashi**tte***
su	→	*-shite*	*hanasu*	*hana**shite***
tsu	→	*-tte*	*matsu*	*ma**tte***
u	→	*-tte*	*narau*	*nara**tte***

For -*ru* verbs change:

| *ru* → -*te* | *miru* | *mite* |
| | *taberu* | *tabete* |

Irregular verbs:

| *iku* | *itte* | *kuru* | *kite* |
| *suru* | *shite* | | |

EXERCISES
1. -Te imasu

Change the following verbs into present continuous tense:

ex. iku
→ *itte imasu*

au	*kiku*
aruku	*kuru*
asobu	*matsu*
benkyō suru	*narau*
dekakeru	*neru*
furu	*nomu*
hairu	*okiru*
okuru	*hanasu*
oshieru	*suru*
ireru	*taberu*
kaeru	*tsutomeru*
kau	*unten suru*
kaku	*yomu*

-Ni noru
To state that one rides in a vehicle, use vehicle + *ni noru. ex. Kuruma-**ni** **norimashita**.* Rode in a car.

Juku
Juku is attended by most Japanese students, especially during junior high and high school. *Juku* generally consists of classes held after school that prepare students for school entrance examinations. *Juku* is very rigorous with many memorization drills. Some students attend *juku* every week night until ten or eleven p.m.

63

**VERBS
(cont.)**
tsukuru(-u)
to make

*tsutomeru
(-ru)*
to work

**ADDITIONAL
WORDS**
ame
rain

chatto
text message

chotto
a little,
moment

dōzo
please

furui(i)
old (things,
not people)

genki(na)
healthy

go-
honorific
prefix

ichinen
one year

ichinenkan
for one year

ikaga
how

iroiro(na)
various

isogashii(i)
busy

2. -Te imasu

Substitute the phrases into the conversation:

> *ex. hon-o yomu*
> A: *Nani-o shite imasu-ka.*
> B: **_Hon-o yonde_** *imasu.*
>
> *Nihongo-o benkyō suru*
> *īmēru-o yomu*
> *rajio-o kiku*
> *sake-o nomu*
> *gohan-o taberu*
> *pen-o kau*
> *aruku*
> *ocha-o ireru*

SHORT DIALOGUES

1. *ex.* terebi-o miru

> Kumiko: *Michiko-san ima isogashii desu-ka.*
> Michiko: *Sukoshi isogashii desu.*
> Kumiko: *Nani-o shite imasu-ka.*
> Michiko: **_Terebi-o mite_** *imasu.*

1. gohan-o taberu   6. sukāto-o kau
2. bīru-o nomu   7. toranpu-de asobu
3. shinbun-o yomu   8. bideo-o miru
4. ocha-o ireru   9. Eigo-o benkyō suru
5. murasaki iro-no kutsushita-o kau

2. *ex.* hon, atarashii, furui

   A: *Anata-no **hon**-wa **atarashii** desu, ne.*
   B: *Iie. Watashi-no **hon**-wa **furui** desu, yo.*

      1. kuruma, hayai, osoi
      2. ie, ōkii, chiisai
      3. sētā, atarashii, furui

3. *ex.* terebi-o miru, Eigo-o benkyō suru

   A: *Hiroko-san.*
   B: *Hai.*
   A: *Ima, **terebi-o mite-imasu**-ka.*
   B: *Iie, **terebi-o mite-imasen. Eigo-o benkyō shite imasu**.*

      1. Okā-san-to hanasu, otō-san-to hanasu
      2. Tōkyō-ni iku, Ōsaka-ni iku
      3. Ame-ga furu, yuki-ga furu
      4. Chatto-o suru, īmēru-o yomu

Iu
Iu is an irregular verb. It is conjugated to *iimasu*. In Hiragana, it is written as *iu*, but sometimes pronounced *yū* in informal situations.

Taihen
Taihen can mean difficult or very, depending on the context. However, do not confuse it with *muzukashii*. *Muzukashii* refers to something that's intellectually difficult to grasp or understand. *Taihen* refers to a difficult situation.

juku
cram school

kara
because,
since

koto
thing

musuko
son

musume
daughter

okamainaku
don't trouble
yourself

sakkā
soccer

sorede
and

sukoshi
a little

taihen(na)
difficult,
tough, very

toranpu
playing cards

wakai(i)
young

yuki
snow

SELF-TEST

Fill in the blanks using *san, wa, ga, o, ni, to, ka* or *de*:

1. Oji _____ _____ eigakan _____ eiga _____ mite imasu.

2. Onii _____ _____ ginkō _____ matte imasu.

3. Keigo _____ _____ Masāki _____ _____ sakkā _____ shite imasu.

4. Ame _____ futte imasu.

5. Michiko _____ _____ doko _____ ocha _____ nonde imasu _____.

Unscramble the following sentences:

6. o unten imasu kanojo akakute wa kuruma hayai shite.

7. imasu ringo o tabete oishii kare wa.

8. o wa imasu watashi naratte Nihongo.

9. shite Michiko san imasen wa o benkyō Eigo.

10. de ni wa iroirona aimashita hito watashi depāto.

LESSON NINE
AGATTE KUDASAI

In this lesson you will learn:

- The -te kudasai verb form
- Plain negative verbs
- Stating minutes

DIALOGUE

I

ジョンソン:　ばいてんは どちら ですか。

たなか:　　　あちら です。こまかい おかねを もって いますか。

ジョンソン:　はい、ひゃく ご じゅう えん ぐらい もって います。
とうきょうに いきます。どの くらい じかんが
かかりますか。

たなか:　　　にじゅうごふん ぐらい かかります。

ジョンソン:　あなたは しごとに いきますか。

たなか:　　　はい、しごとに いきます。

ジョンソン:　どようびと にちようびにも しごとに いきますか。

たなか:　　　ときどき どようびに いきます。にちようびには
いきません。

II

スミス:　ごめん ください。

いまい:　ああ、スミスさん、どうぞ あがって ください。

スミス:　おじゃま します。

いまい:　どうぞ、すわって ください。おちゃを どうぞ。

スミス:　ありがとう ございます。

I	I
Jonson: *Baiten-wa dochira desu-ka.*	Johnson: Which way is the ticket stand?
Tanaka: *Achira desu. Komakai okane-o motte imasu-ka.*	Tanaka: It is over that way. Do you have small change?
J: *Hai, hyaku go jū en*	J: Yes, about 150 yen. I

gurai motte imasu.
Tōkyō-ni ikimasu.
Dono kurai jikan-ga
kakarimasu-ka.

T: *Nijūgofun gurai*
   kakarimasu.

J: *Anata-wa shigoto-ni*
   ikimasu-ka.

T: *Hai, shigoto-ni*
   ikimasu.

J: *Doyōbi-to nichi-*
   yōbi-ni-mo shigoto-
   ni ikimasu-ka.

T: *Tokidoki doyōbi-ni*
   ikimasu. Nichiyōbi-
   ni-wa ikimasen.

II

Sumisu: *Gomen kudasai.*

Imai: *Ā, Sumisu-*
san, dōzo agatte
kudasai.

S: *Ojama shimasu.*

I: *Dōzo, suwatte*
   kudasai. Ocha-o
   dōzo.

S: *Arigatō gozaimasu.*

am going to Tokyo.
About how long will
it take?

T: About 25 minutes.

J: Are you going to
   work?

T: Yes.

J: Do you go there
   also on Saturdays
   and Sundays?

T: Sometimes I go on
   Saturday. I don't go
   on Sundays.

II

Smith: Excuse me.

Imai: Oh, Ms. Smith,
   please come in.

S: I am intruding.

I: Please sit down.
   Please have some
   tea.

S: Thank you very
   much.

Motte
Motte means
"to hold" or "to
have with you."
Therefore, *motte*
itte literally
means "to have
with you when
you go," or
"take." *Motte*
kite means "to
have with you
when you come"
or "bring."

Mo
Mo cannot
replace *ni,*
e or *de.* It is
stated after
these particles.
ex. Doyōbi-ni-
mo shigoto-ni
ikimasu-ka.
Do you also
go to work on
Saturdays?

69

achira
that way

agaru(-u)
to step up,
rise

baiten
ticket/news
stand

dasu(-u)
to take out

dochira
which way

-e
indicates
direction

fun, pun
minutes

geimu
game

**gomen
kudasai**
excuse me

gurai, kurai
approximately,
about

Hiruton
Hilton

jā
well

jikan
time

kaisha
company

GRAMMAR EXPLANATION
1. -Te Kudasai

The verb form -te kudasai is used when requesting someone to please do something.

> ex. Gohan-o **tabete kudasai.**
> Please eat the food.
>
> Kaisha-ni **kite kudasai.**
> Please come to my company.

Once you know how to conjugate verbs to verb + -te imasu, it is very easy to learn the verb + kudasai form. Use the same base verb and add kudasai.

> ex. mite imasu   is looking
> mite **kudasai**   please look
>
> yonde imasu   is reading
> yonde **kudasai**   please read

2. -Nai

To change the plain form of verbs into negative, the following rules apply:

> ru verbs - drop ru and add nai
> taberu   tabe**nai**
> miru   mi**nai**
>
> u verbs - replace the final u with anai:
> iku   ik**anai**
> yomu   yom**anai**

hanasu	*hanas**anai***
wakaru	*wakar**anai***

u verbs with a vowel before *u* - drop *u* and add *wanai*:

iu	*i**wanai***

Exceptions:

kuru	*ko**nai***
suru	*shi**nai***
desu	*dewa **nai**, ja **nai*** (informal)

3. Ni

When **specific** time periods, days, dates, months or years are said to describe when one did or will do something, *ni* always follows.

> ex. *Oku-san-wa nichiyōbi-**ni** Amerika-ni ikimasu.*
> Mr. Oku will go to America on Sunday.
>
> *Hara-san-wa sanji-**ni** uchi-ni kaerimashita.*
> Mr. Hara returned home at 3:00.

However, when you say **general** times such as yesterday, today, tomorrow, last week, last month, last year, last month, etc., *ni* is not used.

> ex. *Yūbe takusan benkyō shimashita.*
> Last night I studied a lot.
>
> *Mainichi īmēru-o shite imasu.*
> Everyday I e-mail. (lit. Everyday I am doing e-mail)

When you drop the *re* from *kore, sore, are* and *dore* then add *chira* to form *kochira, sochira, achira* and *dochira*, the meanings change to "this way" (close to speaker), "that way" (close to listener), "that way" (far from speaker and listener) and "which way." They are also polite words for *kore, sore, are* and *dore*.

E
e can be interchanged with *ni* when indicating direction. *ex. gakko-e ikimasu* or *doko-e ikimasu-ka.*

71

kaijō
meeting place

kakaru(-u)
to require, take

kikan
time period

kippu
ticket

komakai
small change

kudamono
fruit

mainichi
every day

motsu(-u)
to hold, have with you

nigiyaka(na)
lively

ojama shimasu
I am in your way

okane
money

onegai shimasu
I plead with you

reizōko
refrigerator

shigoto
work

EXERCISES
1. -Te kudasai

Change the following verbs into the -te kudasai form:

ex. machimasu
➡ *matte kudasai*

agemasu	aimasu
arukimasu	naraimasu
nomimasu	okimasu
hanashimasu	hashirimasu
yarimasu	kikimasu
kakimasu	tsutomemasu
yomimasu	iremasu
hairimasu	shimasu
tabemasu	oshiemasu

2. Negative plain verbs

Substitute the phrases into the given sentences:

ex. kuruma-o unten suru
    Okā-san: Nobutaka-san-wa
        ***kuruma-o unten suru**-no.*

    Musoko: Iie, Nobutaka-san-wa
        ***kuruma-o unten shinai**.*

asobimasu	enpitsu-o kaimasu
dekakemasu	uchi-ni kimasu
ikimasu	nemasu
kaerimasu	chatto-o suru
Eigo-o naraimasu	
sakkā-ga dekimasu	

3. Minutes

The way to express minutes when telling time is as follows:

1 minute - *ippun*
2 minutes - *nifun*
3 minutes - *sanpun*
4 minutes - *yonpun*
5 minutes - *gofun*
6 minutes - *roppun*
7 minutes - *nanafun*
8 minutes - *happun*
9 minutes - *kyūfun*
10 minutes - *juppun*

This pattern continues regularly until 60.

ex. 6:35 *rokuji sanjūgofun*
9:13 *kuji jūsanpun*

4. Practice saying the following times:

3:15	4:38	10:21
6:47	1:22	12:44
11:06	2:59	

sNo
No can replace *ka* or *yo* in informal speech. *ex. Doko-ni iku-no*. Where do you go?

Business functions and parties in Japan are generally held at hotels or restaurants. Business associates are not often invited into a Japanese home, as homes are considered private.

AGATTE KUDASAI

sochira
that way, that direction

suwaru(-u)
to sit

takusan
much

tariru(-ru)
to be enough

tokidoki
sometimes

tsukeru(-ru)
to turn on

yaru(-u)
to do

yūbe
last night

yūgata
evening
(sunset)

SHORT DIALOGUES

1. *ex.* terebi-o miru, terebi-o tsukeru

Yamada: Nanika shimashō-ka.
Buraun: Hai, ii desu yo.
*Yamada: Jā, **terebi-o mimashō**-ka.*
Buraun: Sō desu, ne. (telephone rings)
*Yamada: Sumimasen. **Terebi-o tsukete** kudasai.*

1. ocha-o nomu, ocha-o ireru
2. kudamono-o taberu, reizōko-kara ringo-o dasu
3. hon-o yomu, hon-o motte kuru
4. bideo-o miru, bideo-o ireru

2. *ex.* omoshiroi, Kyōto-no resutoran, Yamamoto

Imai: Kinyōbi-no pātī-wa dō deshita-ka
*Jonson: **Omoshiroi** pātī deshita. Kaijō-wa **Kyōto-no resutoran** deshita, yo.*
*Imai: Sō desu-ka. **Yamamoto**-san-to hanashimashita-ka.*
Jonson: Hanashimasen deshita. Jikan-ga arimasen deshita yo.

1. nigiyakana, Tōkyō-no hoteru, Kitamura
2. omoshiroi, Shinjuku-no resutoran, Morita
3. nigiyakana, Osaka-no hoteru, Ishibashi

3. *ex.* terebi-o miru, 10

> *Okā-san: Benkyō shite iru-no.*
> *Musuko: Benkyō shite inai, yo.* **_Terebi-o_**
> **_mite iru_**. *no.*
> *Okā-san: Sō. Ato dono gurai* **_miru_**-*no.*
> *Musuko:* **_Juppun_** *gurai.*

   1. hon-o yomu, 15
   2. terebi geimu-o suru, 2
   3. gohan-o taberu, 7
   4. sakkā-o suru, 13

SELF-TEST

Translate the following sentences into Japanese:

1. Please eat the tempura.

2. Please come to my house at about 2:15.

3. Which way is the bank?

4. Please buy a ticket.

5. 2,000 yen is not enough (i.e., You are short 2,000 yen).

6. Is your grandmother healthy?

7. Please wait until 5:39.

8. Do you have small change?

9. Do you go to work everyday?

10. Please come this way.

LESSON TEN
YOKATTA DESU

In this lesson you will learn:

- The past tense of adjectives
- Stating how often an event occurs
- Time periods

DIALOGUE

I

A: ゆうべは ありがとう ございました。

B: どう いたしまして。

A: こんど、わたしの うちに きて ください。いつ おひま ですか。

B: そう ですね。わたしは あたらしい プロジェクトを はじめます
ので らいしゅうは いそがしい です。

A: いつ ごろ おわりますか。

B: らいしゅうの きんようびには おわります。

A: あした いっしょに どこかへ いきましょうか。

A: いいえ、あしたは いち にち じゅう いそがしい です。

B: ざんねん ですね。

II

A: ゆうべの えいがは どう でしたか。

B: えいがは おもしろくて とても よかった です。

A: つきに どの くらい えいがを みますか。

B: つきに いっかい ぐらいは みます。あなたは どう ですか。

A: にかげつに いっかい ぐらいは みます。

B: いつか いっしょに いきましょうか。

A: それは いい ですね。

I

A: *Yūbe-wa arigatō gozaimashita.*

B: *Dō itashimashite.*

A: *Kondo, watashi-no uchi-ni kite kudasai. Itsu o-hima desu-ka.*

B: *Sō desu ne. Watashi-wa atarashii purojekuto-o hajimemasu node, raishū-wa isogashii desu.*

I

A: Thank you very much for (supper) last evening.

B: You're welcome.

A: Next time, please come to my house. When will you be free?

B: Well, I will start a new project, so I will be very busy next week.

A: *Itsu goro owarimasu-ka.*

A: When will you finish it?

B: *Raishū-no kinyōbi-ni-wa owarimasu.*

B: I will finish next Friday.

A: *Ashita issho-ni dokoka-e ikimashō-ka.*

A: Shall we go somewhere tomorrow?

B: *Iie, ashita-wa ichi nichi jū isogashii desu.*

B: No, tomorrow I'm busy all day long.

A: *Zannen desu, ne.*

A: That's too bad.

II

II

A: *Yūbe-no eiga-wa dō deshita-ka.*

A: How was the movie last night?

B: *Eiga-wa omoshiro-kute totemo yokatta desu.*

B: It was interesting and very good.

A: *Tsuki-ni dono kurai eiga-o mimasu-ka.*

A: How many times a month do you see a movie?

B: *Tsuki-ni ikkai gurai-wa mimasu. Anata-wa dō desu-ka.*

B: I usually see one about once a month. How about you?

A: *Nikagetsu-ni ikkai gurai-wa mimasu.*

A: I usually see one about once every two months.

B: *Itsuka issho-ni ikimashō-ka.*

B: Sometime, shall we go together?

A: *Sore-wa ii desu ne.*

A: That would be good.

-Go ni
When stating a change that will occur **after** a specific time period, add *-go ni* to the time frame. *ex. Nishūkan* **go-ni** *Amerika-ni kaerimasu.* I will go back to America in two weeks. However, when talking about a general time frame, such as next week, next month, etc., use *kara* (which means "after" in this case). *ex. Raishū kara, Amerika-ni kaerimasu.* After next week, I will go back to America.

arigatō gozaimashita
thank you for what you did

asagohan
breakfast

asobi-ni
to see someone

da
plain form of desu

dareka
someone

-do
number of times

dokoka
some place, somewhere

goro
approximately, around

hajimeru(-u)
to begin (requires object)

hima
free, available

hiru
noon

hirugohan
lunch

hontō
real, true

GRAMMAR EXPLANATION
1. Adjectives to past tense

In Japanese, when sentences in the past tense contain *i* adjectives directly before a verb, the adjectives are changed instead of the verb.

To change an *i* adjective to past tense, drop the final *i* and add *katta*.

> ex. *Koebi-wa oishii desu.*
> The shrimp is delicious.
>
> *Koebi-wa oishikatta desu.*
> The shrimp was delicious.

Na adjectives stay the same. Change *desu* to *deshita*.

> ex. *Sono onnanohito-wa kirei **desu**.*
> That woman is beautiful.
>
> *Sono onnanohito-wa kirei **deshita**.*
> That woman was beautiful.

2. How Often

The grammar structure for stating how often something occurs is as follows:

(time period) ***kan-ni*** (how often)-***kai/do*** (verb).

> ex. *Isshūkan-ni ni-kai unten shimasu.*
> *Isshūkan-ni ni-do unten shimasu.*
> I drive two times a week.

*Nishūkan-ni san-do taitei resutoran-ni
ikimasu.*
*Nishūkan-ni san-kai taitei resutoran-ni
ikimasu.*
I usually go to a restaurant three times
every two weeks.

3. Issho-ni

Use *to* with *issho-ni* when stating you did or will
do something together with a person or thing.

> ex. *Sumisu-san-wa Tanaka-san-to issho-ni
> ikimashita.*
> Mr. Smith and Mr. Tanaka went together.
>
> *Hara-san-wa watashi-to issho-ni sugu
> benkyō shimasu.*
> Mrs. Hara and I will soon study together.

EXERCISES
1. Adjectives to past tense

Change the following adjectives to past tense:

> ex. *oishii desu*
> ➡ *oishikatta desu*

atsui desu	*hayai desu*
hiroi desu	*omoshiroi desu*
osoi desu	*samui desu*
muzukashii desu	*yasashii desu*

To ask how
many times an
event occurs,
you can use
nando or *nankai*.
ex. *Isshukan-ni
nando sake-o
nomimasu-ka.
Isshukan-ni
nakai sake-o
nomimasu-ka.*
How many times
in one week do
you drink sake?

Kan
Kan states the
time period.
Ishhukan, for
one week.
Ichijikan, for one
hour. *Nishūkan*,
for two weeks.
Sanjuppunkan,
for 30 minutes.

ichi nichi jū
all day long

ikkai
once

issho-ni
together

isshūkan
one week

itsu
when

itsuka
some time

-kai
number of
times

koebi
shrimp

kondo
next time

maiasa
every morning

mata
again

mō
already

-nen
counter for
years

nishūkan
two weeks

node
because,
since (more
polite than
kara)

2. Time periods:

Days

One day - *ichinichi*	Six days - *muika*
Two days - *futsuka*	Seven days - *nanoka*
Three days -*mikka*	Eight days - *yōka*
Four days - *yokka*	Nine days - *kokonoka*
Five days - *itsuka*	Ten days - *tōka*

The additional numbers are the same as used in counting, +*nichi*.
   ex. jūichinichi - 11 days

Weeks
   One week - *isshū*
   Two weeks - *nishū*
   Three weeks - *sanshū*
   Four weeks - *yonshū*
   Five weeks - *goshū*

This pattern continues regularly, number+*shū*.

Months
   One month - *ikkagetsu, tsuki, hitotsuki*
   Two months - *nikagetsu*
   Three months - *sankagetsu*
   Four months - *yonkagetsu*
   Five months - *gokagetsu*

The pattern continues, number + *kagetsu*.
   ex. Ten months - *jukkagetsu*
        Eleven months - *jūikkagetsu*

Years

One year - *ichinen*	Four years - *yonen*
Two years - *ninen*	Five years - *gonen*
Three years - *sannen*	

This pattern continues regularly, number+*nen*.

3. Dates of the month:

first - *tsuitachi*
second - *futsuka*
third - *mikka*
fourth - *yokka*
fifth - *itsuka*
sixth - *muika*
seventh - *nanoka*
eighth - *yōka*
ninth - *kokonoka*
tenth - *tōka*
twentieth - *hatsuka*

The rest of the numbers are stated the same as when counting, plus nichi.
*ex. jūichi**nichi***

To say the date, state the year, month, then day.

ex. nisen hyaku nen shigatsu muika
2100, April 6

Sen kyūhaku kyūjūyo nen kugatsu jūsannichi
1994, September 13

Ichigatsu tsuitachi-wa yasumi desu.
January 1 is a holiday.

Mai
When *mai* is added to the beginning of a word that indicates a day or time, it becomes every ___. *ex. mainichi*, every day. *Maishū*, every week. *Maitsuki*, every month.

When an adjective appears *directly* before a noun and you are speaking in the past tense, change the verb, not the adjective. *ex. omoshiroi pātī deshita.*

owaru(-u)
to finish (no object)

purojekuto
project

raishū
next week

senshū
last week

sugoi(i)
great

sugu
immediately, soon

taitei
usually

tesuto
test

tsuki
one month's time

ukeru(-ru)
to take (a test)

yasumi
holiday, rest time, break time

yūhan
supper

zannen(na)
too bad

4. Practice

State the following times Mr. Smith eats sushi:

ex. once a week
➡ *Sumisu-san-wa **isshū**kan-ni **ichi**-do sushi-o tabemasu.*

once a year, month
twice a year, week, month
three times a year, week, month

SHORT DIALOGUES

1. *ex.* eiga-o, miru, omoshiroi

*Yuki: Sono-**eiga-o mimashita**-ka.*
*Hiroko: Hai, senshū-no kinyōbi-ni **mimashita**.*
Yuki: Dō deshita-ka.
*Hiroko: **Omoshirokatta** desu.*

1. atarashii resutoran-ni, iku, oishii
2. tesuto-o, ukeru, muzukashii
3. atarashii depāto-ni, iku, takai
4. eiga-o, miru, sugoi

2. *ex.* ikkagetsu, eiga-o miru, nikai

> Tanaka: Sumisu-san-wa ***ikkagetsu***-ni
> dono gurai ***eiga-o mimasu***-ka.
> Sumisu: Sō-desu ne. ***Ikkagetsu***-ni ***nikai***
> gurai ***eiga-o mimasu***.
> Tanaka: Hontō desu-ka. Jā, kondo
> issho-ni ikimashō.
> Sumisu: Hai. Sō shimashō.

> 1. isshūkan, eiga-o miru, sankai
> 2. ichinen, Kyōto-ni iku, ichido
> 3. isshūkan, resutoran-de taberu,
>   yonkai
> 4. isshūkan, sake-o nomu, nikai

Rai
Rai is a prefix meaning "next" and is combined with words like week, month and year to form *raishū*, next week, *raigetsu*, next month and *rainen*, next year.

3. *ex.* nishūkan-go-ni, tsuitachi, hirugohan

> Kaori: Kondo itsu aimashō-ka.
> Kumiko: Sō desu ne. ***Nishūkan-go-ni***
> hima desu yo.
> Kaori: Sore dewa, nigatsu ***tsuitachi***-ni
> aimashō-ka.
> Kumiko: Hai. Sō shimashō.
> Kaori: ***Hirugohan***-o issho-ni tabemashō-ka.
> Kumiko: Ii desu yo.

> 1. nishūkan-go-ni, mikka, asagohan
> 2. raishū, kokonoka, yūhan
> 3. raishū, yōka, hirugohan
> 4. sanshūkan-go-ni, futsuka, yūhan

Verbs that are paired with *suru* can be used with *suru* or *-o suru*. *ex.* *unten suru* or *unten-o suru*. Additionally, the first word in the verb pair can stand alone as a noun.

SELF TEST

Use *wa, ga, o, ni, de, do, kai, san, ka* or X in the following blanks:

1. Maiasa _____ Nihongo _____ benkyō shite imasu.

2. Isshūkan _____ san _____ resutoran _____ tabemasu.

3. Watashi _____ nikagetsukan _____ ikkai Kyōto _____ ikimasu.

4. Senshū _____ kinyōbi _____ tesuto _____ muzukashikatta _____ desu.

5. Raishū _____ mokuyōbi _____ shigoto _____ hajimemasu.

Translate the following sentences into Japanese:

6. Friday is not a holiday.

7. I go to the department store once a week.

8. Today is December fifth.

9. On Friday, I took a difficult test.

10. Mr. Tanaka and (I) ate lunch together.

LESSON ELEVEN
IKITAI DESU

In this lesson you will learn:

- How to state wants

- Negative adjectives

- Adverbs

DIALOGUE

I

A: あなたは こうこうせい ですか。

B: はい そう です。

A: ひらかわ けいごくんを しって いますか。

B: ひらかわ けいごくん...

A: かれは せが たかい です。

B: ああ そうそう。かれは わたしの せんぱい です。

A: おねえさんは アメリカで だいがくに はいって いますか。

B: はい はいって います。せんもんは ビジネス です。

A: そう ですか。おねえさんは にほんごも べんきょう して
いますか。

B: まえに にほんごを べんきょう して いた けど もう やめました。
でも かのじょは にほんに いきたいと いって いました。

A: いつ ごろ おねえさんは だいがくを そつぎょう しますか。

B: にねん ぐらいで そつぎょう する かも しれません。

II

A: こんばん げきを みませんか。

B: ああ こんばんの おんがくかいの きっぷが あります。
すっかり わすれて いました。いきませんか。

A: いい ですよ。なんじに はじまりますか。

B: しちじに はじまります。

A: きっぷは たかい ですか。

B: いいえ あまり たかく ありません。

I	**I**
A: *Anata-wa kōkō-sei desu-ka.*	A: Are you a high school student?
B: *Hai, sō desu.*	B: Yes I am.
A: *Hirakawa Keigo-kun-o shitte imasu-ka.*	A: Do you know Keigo Hirakawa?
B: *Hirakawa Keigo-kun . . .*	B: Keigo Hirakawa . . .
A: *Kare-wa se-ga takai desu.*	A: He is tall.

B: Ā, sō sō. Kare-wa watashi-no senpai desu.

A: Onē-san-wa Amerika-de daigaku-ni haitte imasu-ka.

B: Hai, haitte imasu. Senmon-wa bijinesu desu.

A: Sō desu-ka. Onē-san-wa Nihongo-mo benkyō shite imasu-ka.

B: Mae-ni Nihongo-o benkyō shite ita kedo, mō yamemashita. Demo kanojo-wa Nihon-ni ikitai-to itte imashita.

A: Itsu goro onē-san-wa daigaku-o sotsugyō shimasu-ka.

B: Ninen gurai-de sotsugyō suru kamo shiremasen.

II

A: Konban geki-o mimasen-ka.

B: Ā, konban-no ongakukai-no kippu-ga arimasu. Sukkari wasurete imashita. Ikimasen-ka.

A: Ii desu yo. Nanji-ni hajimarimasu-ka.

B: Shichiji-ni hajimarimasu.

A: Kippu-wa takai desu-ka.

B: Iie, amari takaku arimasen.

B: Oh yes, he is ahead of me.

A: Is your older sister in college in America?

B: Yes. Her major is business.

A: Really. Is she also studying Japanese?

B: She was before, but she gave up. However, she said she would like to come to Japan.

A: When will she graduate from college?

B: I'm not sure, but maybe in about 2 years.

II

A: Would you like to see a play tonight?

B: Oh, I have tickets to a concert tonight. I completely forgot about it. Would you like to go?

A: That's fine. What time does it start?

B: It starts at 7:00.

A: Were the tickets expensive?

B: No, not very expensive.

To state that one is working somewhere, say the name of the company or place, then add *-ni tsutomete imasu*. ex. *Tanaka-san-wa Mitsubishi-ni tsutomete imasu.* Mr. Tanaka is working at Mitsubishi. *Watashi-wa toshokan-ni tsutomete imasu.* I am working at a library.

ā, sō sō
Oh, that's right

bijinesu
business

daigaku
college

daredemo
everyone

denshi
electronic

denshi bukku
e-book

dokodemo
everywhere

ga
but

geki
play

gekijō
live theater

hajimaru(-u)
to start (no object)

ita
was (plain)

itsudemo
any time

kamo shirenai
I'm not sure

kedo
but, though

GRAMMAR EXPLANATION
1. -Tai desu

To change verbs to mean "I want to _____,"
drop *masu* and add *tai desu*.

> *ex. Watashi-wa Tōkyō-ni ikimasu.*
> I go to Tokyo.
>
> *Watashi-wa Tōkyō-ni ikitai desu.*
> I want to go to Tokyo.
>
> *Watashi-wa tsugi-ni Supeingo-o benkyō shitai desu.*
> I want to study Spanish next.

When asking someone if they want to do something, Japanese people usually ask using a negative verb.

> *ex. Tōkyō-ni ikimasen-ka.*
> Don't you (want to) go to Tokyo?

2. Negative adjectives

To convert *i* adjectives into negative, drop the final *i* and add *-ku arimasen*.

> *ex. Kono kuruma-wa hayai desu.*
> This car is fast.
>
> *Kono kuruma-wa hayaku arimasen.*
> This car is not fast.
>
> *Kōkō-no benkyō-wa muzukashii desu.*
> High school studies are difficult.

Kōkō-no benkyō-wa muzukashiku arimasen.
High school studies are not difficult.

For informal speech, use *-ku nai*

ex. Kono o-kashi-wa oishiku nai.
This snack is not delicious.

To change *na* adjectives into negative, add *dewa arimasen* after the adjective.

ex. kirei dewa arimasen
not beautiful

genki dewa arimasen
not healthy

For informal speech, use *ja nai*.

ex. taihen ja nai
not tough

3. Adjectives to Adverbs

To change adjectives into adverbs:

For *i* adjectives, drop the final *i* and add *ku*

ex. hayai
hayaku owarimashita
finished quickly

osoi
osoku tabemasu
eats slowly

Hajimeru and *hajimaru*, along with *oeru* and *owaru* are two examples of verbs that have the same meaning, but require different grammar structure. *Hajimeru* and *oeru* need to have objects preceeding them, while *hajimaru* and *owaru* are used without objects. *ex. Itsu owarimashita-ka.* When did you finish? *Itsu purojekuto-o oemashita-ka.* When did you finish the project?

kōhai
one's junior

kōkō
high school

konban
this evening

kono goro
these days

-kun
used instead
of -san at the
end of a boy's
name

kurashikku
classical

nandemo
anything,
everything

oeru(-ru)
to finish (re-
quires object)

ongakukai
concert

se-ga takai
tall

-sei
student
(suffix)

senmon
major

senpai
one's senior

shitte iru
to know

For *na* adjectives, drop the final *na* and add *ni*

> *ex. kirei**na***
> *kirei-**ni** Nihongo-o hanashimasu*
> speaks Japanese beautifully

> *genki**na***
> *genki-**ni** narimasu*
> becomes healthy (better)

Adverbs can come either directly before the verb or the object:

> *ex. kuruma-o **hayaku** unten shimasu*
> ***hayaku** kuruma-o unten shimasu*
> drives the car quickly

> ***kirei-ni** Nihongo-o hanashimasu*
> *Nihongo-o **kirei-ni** hanashimasu*
> speaks Japanese beautifully

4. -Kamo shiremasen

To state that you are unsure about something, use a plain verb, then add -*kamo shiremasen*.

> *ex. Michiko-san-wa Supeingo-o benkyō suru **kamo shiremasen.***
> I'm not sure, (but I think) Michiko studies Spanish.

> *Ashita ame-ga furu **kamo shiremasen.***
> I'm not sure, (but I think) it will rain tomorrow.

EXERCISES

1. Shitai

Place these verbs into the following sentence:

ex. unten suru

➡ *Watashi-wa **unten shitai desu** kedo, mō yamemasu.*

kiku	yaru	kaeru
kaku	kau	yomu
kuru	iku	aruku
matsu	asobu	miru
narau	dekakeru	nomu
tsutomeru	hairu	oshieru
hanasu	suru	hashiru
taberu	benkyō suru	

2. Negative Adjectives

Change the adjectives to negative, then place them in the following sentences:

ex. takai

    *A: Sore-wa **takai** desu-ka.*

    *B: Iie, amari **takaku** arimasen.*

atsui	hayai	osoi
hiroi	samui	muzukashii
omoshiroi	yasashii	oishii
yasui	kurai	furui
taihen(na)	kirei(na)	suki(na)

sotsugyō
suru
to graduate

sukkari
completely

Supeingo
Spanish

-tachi
plural suffix

-to itte
imashita
was saying

toshokan
library

tsugi-ni
next

wasureru
(-ru)
to forget

watashitachi
we

yameru(-ru)
to give up,
stop

zasshi
magazine

zuibun
very

3. Change the adjectives into adverbs when combining them with their paired word:

ex. hayai, unten shimasu
➡ *hayaku unten shimasu*

hayai, hashirimasu	*osoi, narimasu*
yasashii, shimasu	*yoi, nemasu*
akarui, narimasu	*kireina, narimasu*

4. Substitute the following work places into the sentence:

Hanabusa-san-wa _____ -ni tsutomete imasu.

daigaku	*Toyota*	*yūbinkyoku*
biyōin	*depāto*	*Honda*
resutoran	*byōin*	*yakkyoku*

5. -Kamo shiremasen

Change the following sentences into the *-kamo shiremasen* phrase:

ex. Geki-wa shichiji-han-ni hajimarimasu.
➡ ***Geki-wa shichiji-han-ni hajimaru*** *kamo shiremasen.*

Sensei-wa isogashiku arimasen.
Ninenkan Nihongo-o benkyō shite imasu.
Kare-wa watashi-no kōhai desu.
Ano hito-no senmon-wa bijinesu desu
Yagi-san-wa toshokan-ni tsutomete imasu
Kyō Morita-san-wa Tōkyō-ni ikimasen
Ano hito-wa gakusei dewa arimasen.

SHORT DIALOGUES

1. *ex.* hon-o yomu

> A: *Nani-o shitai desu-ka.*
> B: *Nandemo ii desu. Anata-wa.*
> A: ***Hon-o yomitai*** *desu.*
> B: *Jā, sō shimashō.*
>
> 1. oishii tenpura-o tsukuru
> 2. kuruma-o unten suru
> 3. Supeingo-o benkyō suru
> 4. Tōkyō-ni iku
> 5. zubon-o kau
> 6. kurashikku-o kiku

Tachi
When -*tachi*
is added to
certain nouns, it
changes those
words to plural.
*ex. kodomo +
tachi* = children;
*watashi +
tachi* = we/us;
*Yamada-san
+ tachi = Miss
Yamada* and the
others.

2. *ex.* denshi bukku, yomu, omoshiroi

> A: *Sumimasen, osoku narimashite.*
> B: *Ii desu yo. Hirakawa-san-tachi-mo
>   mada kite imasen yo.*
> A: *Tokorode,* ***denshi bukku****-o mō*
>   ***yomimashita****-ka.*
> B: *Hai,* ***yomimashita****.*
> A: *Zuibun hayaku* ***yomimashita****, ne.*
> B: *Ē,* ***omoshirokatta*** *desu kara.*
>
> 1. atarashii zasshi, yomu, omoshiroi
> 2. atarashii purojekuto, oeru, yasashii
> 3. kippu, kau, yasui
> 4. atarashii bideo, miru, omoshiroi

3. *ex.* daigaku, muzukashii

Imai: *Jonson-san-wa gakusei desu-ka.*

*Jonson:Hai. Senshū-kara **daigaku**-ni itte imasu.*

I: *Sō desu-ka. **Muzukashii** desu-ka.*

J: *Iie, amari **muzukashiku** arimasen. Kono goro-wa isogashii desu-ka.*

I: *Iie, amari isogashiku arimasen.*

1. kōkō, yasashii
2. daigaku, isogashii
3. kōkō, muzukashii

SELF-TEST

Translate the following sentences into Japanese:

1. I want to go to Kyoto next week on Thursday.

2. I want to study Japanese three times a week.

3. Please come quickly.

4. I'm not sure, (but I think) he is ahead of me.

5. I'm not sure, (but I think) Mr. Tanaka is not going to the movie theater.

6. Today it is not very cold.

7. Grandfather is not healthy.

8. Do you want to go to a classical concert this evening?

9. That movie was not interesting.

10. I want to work for Fuji Bank.

LESSON TWELVE
DOCHIRA NO HŌ-GA

In this lesson you will learn:

- How to state comparisons
- Superlatives
- The -nasai verb form

DIALOGUE

I

A: いらっしゃいませ。なにを さしあげましょうか。

B: はな もようの ワンピ—スを ください。

A: はい。サイズは いくつ ですか。

B: きゅう です。

A: いそいで いますか。

B: ええ まあ . . .

A: こちらは どう ですか。

B: もっと あかるい いろの ものは ありますか。

A: はい。これと これは どう ですか。どちらが すき ですか。

B: こちらの ほうが きれい です。これを ください。

A: はい ありがとう ございます。

II

A: けさ ごはんを たくさん たべました。でも おなかが
すきました。きっさてんに いきましょう。

B: それは いい ですね。わたしは のどが かわきました。
でも その きっさてんは とても こんで いますよ。

A: ほんとうに こんで いますね。じゃ もっと すいて いる ところを
さがしましょうか。

B: かまいませんよ。

A: つかれましたか。

B: すこし つかれました。

A: わたしは この きっさてんが いちばん すき です。

B: この きっさてんは たかい ですか。

A: じつは この きっさてんは ほかの きっさてん よりも やすい です。

B: それ なら はいりましょう。

I	**I**
A: *Irasshaimase, nani-o sashiagemashō-ka.*	A: Welcome, with what may I help you?
B: *Hana moyō-no wanpīsu-o kudasai.*	B: I would like a floral dress, please.
A: *Hai. Saizu-wa ikutsu desu-ka.*	A: OK, what size do you wear?
B: *Kyū desu.*	B: I am a nine.
A: *Isoide imasu-ka.*	A: Are you in a hurry?

B: *Ē, mā . . .*

A: *Kochira-wa dō desu-ka.*

B: *Motto akarui iro-no mono-wa arimasu-ka.*

A: *Hai. Kore-to kore-wa dō desu-ka. Dochira-ga suki desu-ka.*

B: *Kochira-no hō-ga kirei desu. Kore-o kudasai.*

A: *Hai, arigatō gozaimasu.*

II

A: *Kesa gohan-o takusan tabemashita, demo onaka-ga sukimashita. Kissaten-ni ikimashō.*

B: *Sore-wa ii desu ne. Watashi-wa nodo-ga kawakimashita. Demo, sono kissaten-wa totemo konde imasu, yo.*

A: *Hontō-ni konde imasu, ne. Jā, motto suite iru tokoro-o sagashimashō-ka.*

B: *Kamaimasen, yo.*

A: *Tsukaremashita-ka.*

B: *Sukoshi tsukaremashita.*

A: *Watashi-wa kono kissaten-ga ichiban suki desu.*

B: *Kono kissaten-wa takai desu-ka.*

A: *Jitsu-wa, kono kissaten-wa hoka-no kissaten yori-mo yasui desu.*

B: *Sore nara hairimashō.*

B: Yes, kind of.

A: How about this one?

B: Do you have a brighter colored one?

A: Yes. How about this one or this one? Which do you like?

B: This one is prettier. I'll take it.

A: Yes, thank you.

II

A: I ate a lot for breakfast, but I am hungry. Let's go to a cafe.

B: That sounds good. I'm thirsty. Oh, this one is very crowded.

A: It is very crowded. Well, shall we find a place that's less crowded?

B: I don't mind.

A: Are you tired?

B: A little.

A: This cafe is my favorite!

B: Is this cafe expensive?

A: Actually, it's less expensive than other cafes.

B: In that case, let's go in.

To state "I'm full," use *onaka-ga ippai desu.*

Although *ōkii* and *chiisai* are *i* adjectives, when they are directly in front of the noun they modify, they can also act as *na* adjectives. ex. *Ōkii ringo, ōkina ringo; chiisai tsukue, chiisana tsukue.* Either form is acceptable.

amai(i)
sweet

daijōbu
OK, all right

hana
flower

hontō-ni
indeed, really

ikutsu
how old

ippai(i)
full

**ippan teki-ni
ieba**
generally
speaking

irasshaimase
welcome

isogu(-u)
to be in a
hurry

jitsu-wa
actually

kaimono
shopping

kakeru(-ru)
to wear
(glasses)

kamaimasen
(I) don't mind

karui(i)
light (not
heavy)

GRAMMAR EXPLANATION
1. Comparisons

When both objects of comparison are already known:

Motto

Item-**wa motto** adj. **desu**.

ex. *Kono tesuto-wa **motto** muzukashii desu.*
This test is more difficult.

To inquire:
Motto adj. *mono-ga arimasu-ka.*
Motto yasui mono-ga arimasu-ka.
Do you have a cheaper one?

Mō sukoshi

Item-**wa mō sukoshi** adj **desu**.

ex. *Ippan teki-ni ieba kono gakkō-no tesuto-wa **mō sukoshi** muzukashii desu.*
Generally speaking, this school's test is a little more difficult.

***Mō sukoshi** yasui mono-ga arimasu-ka.*
Do you have one that is a little cheaper?

No hō-ga

Item **no hō-ga** adj **desu**.

ex. *Eigo **no hō-ga** yasashii desu.*
English is easier.

*Sono sumāto fon **no hō-ga** ii desu.*
That smart phone is better.

Yori, yori mo

This is used when both objects have yet to be stated. *Yori mo* is a little stronger.

Item one-*wa* item two *yori* (*mo*) adj *desu*.

Item one is more ___ than the second item.

*ex. Eigo-wa Nihongo **yori mo** yasashii desu.*
English is easier than Japanese.

*Amerika-wa Nihon **yori** hiroi desu.*
America is more spacious than Japan.

2. Dochira no hō-ga

To ask someone whether or not something is older, harder, more expensive, etc., use this sentence pattern:

Item one *to* item two *dewa dochi(ra no hō) -ga* adj. *desu-ka.*

*ex. Kono hon-to sono hon dewa **dochi(ra no hō)-ga** omoshiroi desu-ka.*
Which is more interesting, this book or that book?

*Sono ningyō to ano ningyō-wa **dochi(ra no hō)-ga** kirei desu-ka.*
Which is more beautiful, that doll or that doll?

The subject phrase can be omitted if it is undestood.

*ex. **Dochi(ra no hō)-ga** kirei desu-ka.*
Which is more beautiful?

Kawaku
Kawakimasu means "dry," and *nodo* means "throat." Therefore, *nodo-ga kawakimashita* literally means "my throat is dry," or "I'm thirsty."

In less formal situations, *dochira no hō-ga* can be replaced with *docchi-ga*.

kawaku(-u)
to be dry

kesa
this morning

kissaten
cafe

konde iru
to be crowded

kono aida
the other day

mā
kind of

megane
glasses

mō sukoshi
a little more

mono
thing

motto
more

moyō
print

ningyō
doll

nodo
throat

**onaka-ga
suku(-u)**
to be hungry

sagasu(-u)
to look for

saizu
size

If you are asked a *dochi(ra no hō)-ga* question, you must answer in the *(no hō)-ga* form.

If you are asked *dochi(ra no hō)-ga hoshii desu-ka*, and it makes no difference to you, answer *dochi(ra) mo ii desu*, "either one is good."

3. Superlatives

To state that something is the biggest, most expensive, best, etc., use *ichiban+* the adjective. As learned previously, *ichiban* means "number one;" therefore, when you state *ichiban ōkii*, you are literally stating "number one big" or "biggest."

ex. ***ichiban*** *kirei*
prettiest

ichiban *muzukashii*
most difficult

ichiban *suki*
my favorite, what I like best

ichiban *karui*
lightest

4. -Nasai

To command or order someone to do something, only the verb needs to be changed. To do this, drop the ending *masu*, and add **nasai**.

ex. suwarimasu	sits
suwarinasai	sit down!
koko-ni kinasai	come here!

102

EXERCISES

1. No hō-ga

Using the following combination of words, create questions and answers using the *no hō-ga* phrase:

ex. *daigaku, kōkō, taihen*
- A: ***Daigaku*** to ***kōkō****-dewa dochira no hō-ga **taihen** desu-ka.*
- B: ***Daigaku*** *no hō-ga **taihen** desu.*

Nihongo, Eigo, muzukashii
sushi, tenpura, oishii
Toyota-no kuruma, Nissan-no kuruma, hayai
Nihon, Amerika, hiroi
kono o-kashi, sono o-kashi, amai

2. Substitute the given words into the following phrases based on your opinions:

_____-wa _____ yori muzukashii desu.

_____-wa _____ yori yasashii desu.

Eigo, Nihongo
Nihongo, Supeingo
shigoto, benkyō
katakana, hiragana

_____-wa _____ yori motto omoshiroi desu.

kōkō, daigaku
sakkā, yakyū
tanjōbi-no pātī, shigoto-no pātī
eiga, ongakukai

Japanese television commercials generally do not contain comparisons between products. However, sales people usually can feel free to make comparisons between their products and other items.

103

sore nara
in that case

suite iru
not crowded,
to be empty

sumāto fon
smart phone

sunde iru
live

tanjōbi
birthday

tatsu(-u)
to stand

**tsukare-
mashita**
tired

uru(-u)
to sell

yakyū
baseball

yori (mo)
more than

zutto
much

_____-wa _____ yori mō sukoshi takai desu.
　　ocha, kōhī
　　sushi, o-sashimi
　　budōshu, bīru
　　pan, gohan

3. Substitute the following verbs into the sentence using the -nasai form:

ex. gohan-o tabemasu
➡ Nobutaka-kun, **gohan-o tabenasai**.

tomodachi-ni ageru
gakkō-ni iku
aruku
miru
kiku
benkyō suru
koko-de matsu
dekakeru
miruku-o nomu
okiru
uchi-ni hairu
megane-o kakeru
hanasu
yomu
isu-ni suwaru
tatsu
hashiru
kaku
baiten-de kippu-o kau

SHORT DIALOGUES

1. *ex.* onaka-ga sukimashita, taberu, kudamono

A: ***Onaka-ga sukimashita***, *ne.*
B: *Watashi-mo sō desu yo.*
A: *Nanika **tabemashō**-ka.*
B: *Hai.* ***Kudamono**-wa dō desu-ka.*
A: ***Kudamono**-o **tabemashō**.*

   1. nodo-ga kawakimashita, nomu, jūsu
   2. onaka-ga sukimashita, taberu, o-kashi
   3. nodo-ga kawakimashita, nomu, bīru
   4. onaka-ga sukimashita, taberu, sushi

Although *shitte iru* means that one knows something, to state that one does **not** know something, *shirimasen* is always used. The Japanese do not say *shitte imasen.*

2. *ex.* takai

A: *Anata-wa doko-ni sunde imasu-ka.*
B: *Mae-ni Ōsaka-ni sunde imashita.*
  Ima-wa Tōkyō-no apāto-ni sunde imasu.
A: *Dochira no hō-ga **takai** desu-ka.*
B: *Tōkyō-no apāto no hō-ga zutto*
  ***takai** desu.*
A: *Sō desu-ka.*

   1. chiisai
   2. hiroi
   3. yasui
   4. suki

3. *ex.* chiisai, ōkina

Sumisu: Sumimasen, kono kutsu-wa **chiisai** *desu. Motto* **ōkina** *kutsu-ga arimasu-ka.*

Ten'in: Chotto matte kudasai. Ā, arimashita.

Sumisu: Kono kutsu no hō-ga ii desu. Kore-o kudasai.

Ten'in: Hai, arigatō gozaimasu.

1. takai, yasui
2. ōkii, chiisai
3. iro-ga kurai, akarui iro-no
4. iro-ga akarui, kurai iro-no

SELF TEST

Unscramble the following sentences:

1. dewa dochira no Ōsutoraria ka Nihon ga to desu hō hiroi.

2. wa konde kissaten imasu totemo ne kono.

3. ano desu wa takai tatemono ichiban.

4. ōkina hoshii sēta ga motto desu.

5. mo desu hiragana kantan yori.

Fill in the blanks with *wa, ga, de, o, ni, to, no, ka, ne,* or X:

6. Kono ningyō ___ hoka ___ ningyō ___ yori ___ takai desu.

7. Sono eiga ___ ano eiga ___ dochira ___ hō ___ omoshiroi desu ___ .

8. Kono saizu ___ hō ___ ōkii ___ desu.

9. Watashi ___ motto ___ ōkina sētā ___ kaitai desu.

10. Motto ___ akarui iro ___ mono ___ arimasu ___ .

LESSON THIRTEEN
ITTA-TO OMOIMASU

In this lesson you will learn:

- The plain past verb form

- The -to omoimasu phrase

- Noun phrases

DIALOGUE

A: あなたの せんもんは なんですか。

B: こうがくを べんきょう して います。

A: こうがくは にんきが ありますね。

B: はい にんきが あります。

A: エンジニアは いつも ざんぎょう しませんか。

B: いいえ ほとんどの にほんじんが ざんぎょう して いると
おもいますよ。あなたの せんもんは なんですか。

A: ほうりつを べんきょう して います。それ から しゅうしを とりたいと
おもいます。

B: そう ですか。あそこに すわって いる ひとも ほうりつを べんきょう
して います。

A: ああ。あの ひとは もりさん ですね。たぶん あの ひとは わたしの
せいじがくの クラスに はいって いると おもいます。

B: もりさんと いっしょに すわって いる ひとが みえますか。

A: コーヒーを のんで いる ひと ですか。

B: そう です。あの ひとは だいがくいんの がくせい ですよ。

A: そう ですか。

B: はい。かのじょは きょうじゅに なると おもいます。

A: すごい ですね。

A: *Anata-no senmon-wa nandesu-ka.*

A: What's your major?

B: *Kōgaku-o benkyō shite imasu.*

B: I'm studying engineering.

A: *Kōgaku-wa ninki-ga arimasu, ne.*

A: Engineering is popular, isn't it.

B: *Hai, ninki-ga arimasu.*

B: Yes. It's popular.

A: *Enjinia-wa itsumo zangyō shimasen-ka.*

A: Don't engineers have to work a lot of overtime?

B: *Iie, hotondo-no Nihonjin-ga zangyō shite iru-to omoimasu yo. Anata-no sen-mon-wa nandesu-ka.*

B: I think almost all Japanese workers work overtime. What is your major?

A: *Hōritsu-o benkyō shite imasu. Sore kara, shūshi-o toritai-to omoimasu.*

A: I'm studying law. After that, I think I want to get my master's degree.

B: *Sō desu-ka. Asoko-ni suwatte-iru hito-mo hōritsu-o benkyō shite imasu.*

B: Really. That person sitting over there is also studying law.

A: *Ā. Ano hito-wa Mori-san desu, ne. Tabun ano hito-wa watashi-no seijigaku-no kurasu-ni haitte iru-to omoimasu.*

A: Oh, that's Mr. Mori, isn't it? I think he is in my political science class.

B: *Mori-san-to issho-ni suwatte iru hito-ga miemasu-ka.*

B: Do you see the person he's sitting with?

A: *Kōhī-o nonde iru hito desu-ka.*

A: The person drinking coffee?

B: *Sō desu. Ano hito-wa dai-gakuin-no gakusei desu yo.*

B: Yes. She is a graduate student.

A: *Sō desu-ka.*

A: Really.

B: *Hai. Kanojo-wa kyōju-ni naru-to omoimasu.*

B: Yes. I think she will become a professor.

A: *Sugoi desu, ne.*

A: That is great.

Omoimasu
Many times when Japanese people express that they want to do something, they often say *tabun* at the beginning of a sentence and add *-to omoimasu* at the end to soften the statement.

109

anna
that kind of

chūgakkō
middle school

daigakuin
graduate
school

donna
what kind of

enjinia
engineer

hotondo
almost all

ima kara
from now

itsumo
always

jibiki, jisho
dictionary

kinmujikan
working hours

konna
this kind of

kore kara
from here,
from now

kurasu
class

mieru(-ru)
can see

ninki-ga aru
is popular

GRAMMAR EXPLANATION

1. Plain past verbs

To conjugate verbs into the plain past form, use
the same rules as the -te imasu and -te kudasai
forms, but add -ta or -tta instead of -te or -tte.

ex. *itte kudasai*   please go
    itta   went

    hanashite kudasai please speak
    hanashita   spoke

The plain past form of *desu* is *datta*.

2. -To omoimasu

To tell someone what you are thinking, change
the verb in the sentence to the plain present or
plain past form, and add -to omoimasu.

  ex. *Morita-san-wa daigaku-ni ikimasu.*
    Mr. Morita goes to the university.

    *Morita-san-wa daigaku-ni **iku-to omoimasu.***
    I think Mr. Morita goes to the university.
    *Morita-san-wa daigaku-ni **ikanai-to
omoimasu.***
    I think Mr. Morita does not go to the
university.

    *Morita-san-wa daigaku-ni **itta-to omoimasu.***
    I think Mr. Morita went to the university.

When using the -tai verb form, drop *desu* and add *-to omoimasu*.

ex. *Konna daigaku-ni* **hairitai-to omoimasu.**
I think I would like to enter this kind of university.

na adjectives require a verb before *-to omoimasu*.

ex. *Kono tanjōbi-no pātī-wa* **nigiyaka da-to omoimasu.**
I think this birthday party is lively.

Tanjōbi-no pātī-wa **nigiyaka datta-to** *omoimasu.*
I think the birthday party was very lively.

i adjectives do not require a verb before *-to omoimasu*.

ex. *Watashi-wa rekishi-ga* **omoshiroi-to** *omoimasu.*
I think history is interesting.

Yamashita-san-no uchi-wa **hirokatta-to** *omoimasu.*
I think Mr. Yamashita's home was spacious.

Kara
Kara also means "since."
ex. *Nihon-ni kita toki* **kara**, *Nihongo-o benkyō shite imasu.*
Since (the time) I came to Japan, I have been studying Japanese. When paired with *mae* to form *mae kara*, the meaning is "since that time." ex. *gonen* **mae kara,** since five years ago; *nishūkan* **mae kara,** since two weeks ago.

To summarize:

Subject+*wa* object +

         i adj or *i* adj + **katta**
   or   *na* adj + **da** or **datta**
   or   plain verb

              + **-to omoimasu**

omou(-u)
to think

oyogu(-u)
to swim

rāmen
noodles

shitsurei shimasu
I am in your way

shōgakkō
elementary school

sonna
that kind of

supōtsu
sports

tabun
perhaps

toki
a certain time

yūmei(na)
famous

zangyō
overtime

3. Noun Phrases:

Place-*no* preposition-*ni* plain verb ➡ noun

ex. Onnanohito-wa watashitachi-no mae-ni suwatte imasu.
A woman is sitting in front of us.

Watashitachi-no mae-ni suwatte iru onnanohito-wa *Yamashita-san-no oku-san desu.*
The woman sitting in front of us is Mr. Yamashita's wife.

Kuruma-no naka-ni iru hito-wa *sensei dewa nai-to omoimasu.*
I think the person in the car is not a teacher.

Object-*o* plain verb ➡ noun

ex. Otokonohito-wa megane-o kakete imashita.
A man was wearing glasses.

Megane-o kakete ita otokonohito-wa *Sumisu-san deshita.*
The man wearing glasses was Mr. Smith.

Sushi-o tabete iru hito-wa akarui hito desu.
The person eating sushi is a bright (fun) person.

4. Dare-mo kimasen

The interrogative nouns *nani, dare,* and *doko,*

used with *-mo* and verb + *masen* mean "not any," "no one," and "nowhere."

> *ex. Watashi-wa nani-**mo** kai**masen** deshita.*
> I bought nothing.
>
> *Dare-**mo** ki**masen**.*
> No one comes.
>
> *Doko-ni-**mo** iki**masen** deshita.*
> I went nowhere.

EXERCISES

1. Plain past

Change the verbs in the following phrases to reflect plain past tense:

> *ex. Amerika-ni iku*
> *Amerika-ni itta*

purojekuto-o oeru	*tesuto-ga owaru*
Amerika-ni sunde iru	*rāmen-o taberu*
oyogu	*shigoto-ni kuru*
jisho-o kau	*kodomo-wa asobu*
watashi-wa yameru	*kuruma-ni noru*
Chatto-o suru	

2. -To omoimasu

Place the following sentences into the *-to omoimasu* pattern:

> *ex. Yamashita-san-wa daigaku-de yakyū-o shimasu.*
> ➡ ***Yamashita-san-wa daigaku-de yakyū-o suru****-to omoimasu.*

College Life
The four years spent in college is usually the most enjoyable time in a Japanese person's life. The majority of Japanese students spend three to six years preparing for college entrance examinations. However, once they enter a university, they only need to spend a minimal amount of time studying in order to graduate.

113

UNIVERSITY TERMS

bungaku
literature

gakui
4 year degree

hakushi
Ph.D.

hōritsu
law

igaku
medical science

kagaku
science

kōgaku
engineering

kyōju
professor

kyōshitsu
classroom

rekishi
history

seijigaku
political science

shakaigaku
sociology

shinrigaku
psychology

shūshi
master's degree

shūshi-o toru
get a master's degree

Plain verb-to omoimasu

Hanabusa-san-wa yūmeina hito desu.

Gakkō-de iroirona supōtsu-o shimasu.

Rekishi-no hon-o yonde iru hito-wa kyōju desu.

Kanojo-wa Nihon-ni kita toki kara, seijigaku-o benkyō shite imasu.

Nihon-no shokuji-wa amari takaku arimasen.

Adjective -to omoimasu

Kono o-kashi-wa amai desu.

Karei-wa karakatta desu.

Rāmen-wa oishikatta desu.

Kono hon-wa yūmei desu.

Juku-wa totemo taihen deshita.

-Tai-to omoimasu

Igaku-o benkyō shitai desu.

Shūshi-o totta kara, Amerika-ni ikitai desu.

Uchi-de gohan-o tabetai desu.

Plain negative-to omoimasu

Konban-no pātī-ni dare-mo kimasen.

Tōkyō-de nani-mo kaimasen.

Yamashita-san-wa daigaku-de yakyū-o shimasen.

Hirakawa-san-wa ocha-o iremasen.

3. Substitute the given words into the following phrase:

ex. Tonari-ni suwaru

➡ **Tonari-ni suwatte iru** hito-wa daigaku-de benkyō shite imasu.

ningyō-o kau   kōhī-o nomu
yakyū-o suru   asoko-no mise-ni iru
oyogu   shinrigaku-no hon-o yomu
Hara-san-no mae-ni suwaru

SHORT DIALOGUES

1. *ex.* benkyō suru, bungaku

A: *Anata-wa nani-o* **benkyō shitai** *desu-ka.*
B: **Bungaku**-*o* **benkyō shitai**-*to omoimasu.*
A: **Bungaku**-*wa muzukashii desu-ka.*
B: *Iie, amari muzukashiku nai-to omoimasu.*

   1. benkyō suru, hōritsu
   2. yomu, igaku-no hon
   3. benkyō suru, kōgaku
   4. yomu, seijigaku-no hon

2. *ex.* kippu-o kau, kyōju

A: *Asoko-de* **Kippu-o katte iru** *hito-wa Yamashita-san desu-ka.*
B: *Ē, Yamashita-san desu.*
A: *Yamashita-san-wa* **kyōju** *desu-ka.*
B: *Ē,* **kyōju** *da-to omoimasu.*

   1. shinbun-o yomu, Fuji ginkō-no hito
   2. ocha-o nomu, sensei
   3. nanika kau, Mitsubishi ginkō-no hito
   4. isu-ni suwaru, Toyota-no hito
   5. denwa-o kakeru, Honda-no hito

-Ni naru
If a person will become something like a teacher, a professor, a doctor, etc., use *noun+ni naru*. *ex. sensei-***ni** **naru**, become a teacher.

115

3. *ex.* kore kara, toshokan, rekishi

A: *Kore kara, dokoka-e ikimasu-ka.*

B: *Kyōju-to hanashitai node, daigaku-ni ikimasu.*

A: *Sore kara uchi-ni kaerimasu-ka.*

B: *Hai. Uchi-ni kaeru-to omoimasu. Anata-wa.*

A: *Kore kara toshokan-ni ikimasu.*
Asoko-de rekishi-no hon-o yomimasu.
Sore kara, doko-ni mo ikimasen.

B: *Sore dewa, shitsurei shimasu.*

1. kore kara, uchi, shakaigaku
2. ima kara, toshokan, shinrigaku
3. kore kara, kissaten, kagaku
4. ima kara, uchi, seijigaku

SELF TEST

Translate the following sentences into Japanese:

1. I think Mr. Mori read the psychology book.

2. I thought he studied engineering.

3. The woman sitting behind me is eating rice.

4. The man reading a book is Mr. Johnson.

5. The woman driving the car is from Tokyo.

Fill in the blanks with *wa, ga, de, o, ni, to, no, ka, ne,* or X:
6. Isshūkan ___ ikkai ___ shinrigaku ___ kyōshitsu ___ ikimasu.

7. Sushi ___ tabete iru ___ hito ___ sensei ___ naru ___ omoimasu.

8. Yamada-san ___ ushiro ___ suwatte iru ___ hito ___ Mori-san desu.

9. Megane ___ kakete iru ___ hito ___ sensei desu.

10. Tanaka-san ___ daigaku ___ iroirona supōtsu ___ shita ___ omoimasu.

LESSON FOURTEEN
MITA KOTO-GA ARIMASU-KA

In this lesson you will learn:

- The -koto-ga aru phrase
- The -no desu verb form
- How to refer to a third person's wants
- Subject phrases

DIALOGUE

I

A: ジョギングを するのには いい ひ ですね。

B: そう ですね。

A: あそこの ちょうぞうは どんな ちょうぞう ですか。

B: だいぶつ です。

A: あの だいぶつは りっぱ です。

B: そう ですね。べつの だいぶつを みた ことが ありますか。

A: しゃしんを みた だけ です。

B: わたしは もう やめます。きお つけて。

A: はい。

II

A: なんの しゃしんを みて いるの ですか。

B: せんしゅう きゅうかで なえばに いきました。その ときの
しゃしんを みて います。みませんか。

A: はい。この しゃしんは スキーを して いる ところ ですね。
スキーを するのは あぶないと おもいませんか。

B: いいえ。スキーを するのは あぶなく ないと おもいます。
あなたは スキーを した ことが ありますか。

A: いいえ。でも わたしの むすめは とても いきたがって います。

B: おちゃを いかが ですか。

A: はい ありがとう ございます。

I	**I**
A: *Jogingu-o suru-no-ni-wa ii hi desu, ne.*	A: It's a nice day to jog, isn't it.
B: *Sō desu, ne.*	B: Yes, it is.
A: *Asoko-no chōzō-wa donna chōzō desu-ka.*	A: What kind of statue is that over there?
B: *Daibutsu desu.*	B: It's a Buddah statue.
A: *Ano daibutsu-wa rippa desu.*	A: That Buddah statue is impressive.

B: *Sō desu ne. Betsu-no daibutsu-o mita koto-ga arimasu-ka.*

B: Yes, it is. Have you ever seen another Buddah statue?

A: *Shashin-o mita dake desu.*

A: I have only seen pictures.

B: *Watashi-wa mō yame-masu. Kio tsukete.*

B: I will quit now. Be careful.

A: *Hai.*

A: OK.

II

II

A: *Nanno shashin-o mite iru-no desu-ka.*

A: What kind of pictures are you looking at?

B: *Senshū kyūka-de Naeba-ni ikimashita. Sono toki-no shashin-o mite imasu. Mimasen-ka.*

B: Last week we went on vacation to Naeba. I'm looking at those pictures. Would you like to look?

A: *Hai. Kono shashin-wa sukī-o shite iru tokoro desu, ne. Sukī-o suru-no-wa abunai-to omoimasen-ka.*

A: Yes. This picture is of a skiing place, isn't it. Don't you think skiing is dangerous?

B: *Iie, sukī-o suru-no-wa abunaku nai-to omoimasu. Anata-wa sukī-o shita koto-ga arimasu-ka.*

B: No, I think that skiing is not dangerous. Have you ever been skiing?

A: *Iie, demo watashi-no musume-wa totemo ikitagatte imasu.*

A: No, but my daughter really wants to go.

B: *Ocha-o ikaga desu-ka.*

B: Would you like some tea?

A: *Hai, arigatō gozaimasu.*

A: Yes, thank you.

A plain verb followed by *dake desu* means "only." *ex. Ringo-o katta **dake desu**.* I only bought an apple.

Since Japan is a very small, densely populated country, many people do not rely on cars for transportation. The mass transit system in Japan is excellent, so many travel by bus or train.

abunai(i)
dangerous

anzen(na)
safe

benri(na)
convenient

betsu-no
other

boku
I (informal, male)

bun
sentence

chizu
map

chokorēto
chocolate

(chō)zō
statue

daibutsu
statue of buddah

dake
only

dekiru(-ru)
to turn out

densha
train

fasshon
fashion

hi
day

hoshigaru(-u)
another person wants

GRAMMAR EXPLANATION
1. Koto-ga(wa) arimasu-ka

To ask someone if they have ever done something, the sentence pattern is as follows:

Subject-*wa* obj.+plain past verb+*koto-ga(wa)*
arimasu-ka

ex. Jonson-san-wa karei-o tabeta koto-ga arimasu-ka.
Mr. Johnson, have you ever eaten curry?

There are two ways to answer affirmatively:
Hai, karei-o tabeta koto-ga arimasu.
Hai, arimasu.
Yes, I have eaten curry.

To answer negatively:
Iie, karei-o tabeta koto-ga arimasen.
Iie, arimasen.
No, I have never eaten curry.

ex. Sumisu-san-wa Nihon-ni itta koto-wa arimasu-ka.
Mr. Smith, have you ever been to Japan?

Hai, Nihon-ni itta koto-ga arimasu.
Hai, arimasu.
Yes, I have been to Japan.

Iie, Nihon-ni itta koto-wa arimasen.
Iie, arimasen.
No, I have never been to Japan.

2. -No desu

To use this form, use a plain verb+*no desu*.

ex. *taberu-**no desu***   eat, will eat

    *tabeta-**no desu***   ate

    *bun-o **kaite iru-no desu***

    is writing a sentence

    *bun-o **kaite ita-no desu***

    was writing a sentence

In less formal situations, *-n desu* can be used:

ex. *taberu-**n desu***   *tabeta-**n desu***

Da, the plain form of *desu*, changes into *na* when preceding *-no desu* or *-n desu*.

ex. *Akachan-wa onnanoko da.*

    The baby is a girl.

    *Akachan-wa onnanoko **na-no desu.***

    The baby is a girl!

    *Sugoi o-tera **na-no desu.***

    It is a great temple!

Adjectives

For *i* adjectives, use the adjective+*-no desu* or *-n desu*.

ex. *sugoi desu*   is great

    *sugoi-**no desu***   is great!

    *sugoi-**n desu***   is great!

    *sugokatta-**no desu***   was great!

    *sugokatta-**n desu***   was great!

    *sugoku nai-**no desu*** was NOT great

    *sugoku nai-**n desu***   was NOT great

The *-no desu* form of verbs is the same in meaning as the *masu* form, but it is more expressive. When used as a statement, the speaker may be surprised, excited, etc. The one who uses it as a question often wants an explanation. For example, if a mother saw her child going out after she told him not to, she would say *doko-ni iku-no desu-ka*, instead of *doko-ni ikimasu-ka.*

hoshii
want

ikaga desu-ka
How about that? Do you like that?

iyahōn
earphones

jogingu suru
to jog

kamera
camera

kio tsukete
be careful, use good judgement, take care

kotoba
word

kyūka
vacation

moderu
model

Naeba
a ski resort in Japan

nanno
what kind of

ongaku
music

rippa(na)
impressive

sā
well

Na adjectives require *na* before *-no desu* or *-n desu*, except when they are past tense or negative.

ex. *genki desu* — is healthy
genkina-no desu — is healthy!
genkina-n desu — is healthy!
genki datta-no desu — was healthy!
genki datta-n desu — was healthy!
genki dewa nai-no desu — is NOT healthy
genki ja nai-n desu — is NOT healthy

3. -Gatte imasu

When referring to a third person's wants, drop the *i* from *-tai desu* and add *-gatte imasu*. However, if you are asking the person directly, use the negative verb form.

ex. *Anata-wa ongaku-o kikimasen-ka.*
Do you want to listen to music?

*Kare-wa ongaku-o kikita**gatte imasu**.*
He wants to listen to music.

*Watashi-wa chizu-o mi**tai desu**.*
I want to look at the map.

*Kitamura-san-wa chizu-o mita**gatte imasu**.*
Mrs. Kitamura wants to look at the map.

In phrases, it comes directly before the noun it modifies:

ex. *Tanaka-san-ga shashin-o **toritagatte iru** moderu-wa asoko-ni imasu.*
The model that Mrs. Tanaka wants to take a picture of is over there.

Sumisu-san-ga yomitagatte ita zasshi-wa kore desu-ka.
Is this the magazine that Mr. Smith wanted to read?

4. Subject Phrases

When using a verb as a subject phrase use:

object+plain verb *no-wa*

ex. Nihongo-no kotoba-o narau
Nihongo-no kotoba-o narau no-wa *muzukashii desu.*
Learning Japanese words is difficult.

*Amerika-de **shūshi-o toru no-wa** ninki-ga arimasu.*
In America, getting a master's degree is popular.

EXERCISES

1. Koto-ga arimasu

Substitute the given words into the following sentences to form the *koto-ga arimasu* phrase:

ex. daibutsu-o miru
➡ *Sumusi-san-wa **daibutsu-o mita** koto-ga arimasu-ka.*
➡ *Hai, **daibutsu-o mita** koto-ga arimasu.*
➡ *Iie, **daibutsu-o mita** koto-ga arimasen.*

o-tera-ni iku	o-kashi-o tsukuru
shashin-o toru	sukī-o suru
shinrigaku-no hon-o yomu	
Nihon-no fasshon zasshi-o yomu	

Another way to say that you want something is object+*ga hoshii desu.* ex. iyahōn-**ga hoshii desu.** I want earphones.

In English, we say "listen to ear phones," but the Japanese use *suru* with *iyahōn*, not *kiku*.

sakki
a short time
ago

shashin
picture

shukudai
homework

sukī-o suru
to ski

(o)tera
temple

toru(-u)
to take; get

tsukau(-u)
to use

zenzen
(not) at all

2. -Gatte imasu

Substitute the phrases into the following sentence:

ex. Nihon-ni kitai desu

➡ *Sumisu-san-wa **Nihon-ni kitagatte iru**-to omoimasu.*

sukī-o naraitai desu

shashin-o toritai desu

densha-ni noritai desu

kagaku-o benkyō shitai desu

rāmen-o tabetai desu

shūshi-o toritai desu

shōgakkō-ni tsutometai desu

baiten-de kippu-o kaitai desu

asagohan-o tabetai desu

3. Match the following phrases:

1. *Kono kamera-de*
2. *Anata-wa jogingu shita*
3. *Boku-wa omoshiroi zasshi-o*
4. *Kare-wa rajio-o*
5. *Anata-wa hōritsu-o*
6. *Sono ongakukai-wa*
7. *Daigaku-wa amari*

a. *koto-ga arimasu-ka.*
b. *taihen ja nai-no desu.*
c. *shashin-o toru-no desu-ka.*
d. *benkyō shinai-no desu-ka.*
e. *kiku-no desu.*
f. *omoshiroi-no desu.*
g. *yomu-n desu, yo.*

4. Subject Phrases

Change the following verbs into subject phrases:

ex. Jogingu suru, taihen

➡ ***Jogingu suru** no-wa **taihen** desu, ne.*

juku-de benkyō suru, muzukashii

chizu-o miru, yasashii

shashin-o toru, kantan

omoshiroi ie-o kau, taihen

apāto-ni sunde iru, benri
geki-o miru, omoshiroi
shukudai-o suru, taihen

SHORT DIALOGUES

1. *ex.* sushi-o tsukuru, muzukashii, kantan da

Yagi: *Buraun-san-wa,__sushi-o tsukutta__*
koto-ga arimasu-ka.
Buraun: *Hai.* __Sushi-o tsukutta__ *koto-ga arimasu.*
Yagi: __Muzukashikatta__ *desu-ka.*
Buraun: *Iie.* __Sushi-o tsukuru__*-no-wa*
__kantan da__*-to omoimasu.*

   1. seijigaku-o benkyō suru, muzukashii, yasashii
   2. sukī-o suru, yasashii, taihen da
   3. daigakuin-de Nihongo-o narau, muzukashii, yasashii

2. *ex.* zubon, zubon-ga hoshii

Okā-san: *Murasaki iro-no* __zubon__*-to akai*
__zubon__ *dewa dochira no hō-ga* __hoshii__
desu-ka.
Jun: *Boku-wa akai* __zubon-ga hoshii__ *desu.*
Okā-san(ten'in-ni): *Sore dewa akai* __zubon__*-o*
kudasai.
Ten'in: *Hai, arigatō gozaimasu.*

   1. kutsu, kutsu-o kaitai
   2. kami, kami-ga hoshii
   3. kōto, kōto-o kaitai
   4. shatsu, shatsu-ga hoshii

In Japan, American visitors may be surprised by the layout of the towns and cities. Since Japan is such an old country, its streets and roads were not logically planned out ahead of time. If you are in an unfamiliar area, it is very easy to become lost because the roads twist around in many directions, and many roads do not have names. Additionally, when a person gives directions in Japan, he/she will not use road names (*ex.* go to Main Street and turn right), but instead use landmarks (go past the very large tree).

3. *ex.* doko-ni iku, gakkō-ni iku

*Tomoe: Jun-san, **doko-ni iku**-no desu-ka.*
*Jun: **Gakkō-ni iku**-no desu.*
Tomoe: Isogu-no desu-ka.
Jun: Iie, isoide imasen, yo.

1. nani-o taberu, chokorēto-o taberu
2. nani-o suru, shukudai-o suru
3. nani-o nomu, jūsu-o nomu
4. nani-o yomu, shakaigaku-no hon-o yomu
5. dare-to hanasu, tomodachi-to hanasu
6. nani-o suru, shashin-o toru

SELF TEST

Translate the following sentences into Japanese:

1. Have you ever read a Japanese magazine?

2. Have you ever met Naomi?

3. That statue of Buddah is very impressive.

4. Please be careful.

5. The baby is walking!

6. What kind of map is that?

7. He is skiing!

8. Have you ever used this kind of smart phone?

9. She received her four year degree.

10. Kanji is more difficult than hiragana.

LESSON FIFTEEN
DOITSU-NI ITTA TOKI

In this lesson you will learn:

- The -toki noun phrase

- The -shinagara verb phrase

- How to quote others

- Subject phrases

DIALOGUE

I

スミス: もりたさんは ぼうえき がいしゃに つとめて いると ききました。

もりた: そう です。いろいろな ものを ゆしゅつ して います。
ヨーロッパや アメリカに たくさん ゆしゅつ して います。

スミス: ほかの くにへ よく しゅっちょう しますか。

もりた: ええ。きょねん ドイツへ いきました。

スミス: どの くらい たいざい したの ですか。

もりた: さんしゅうかん です。ドイツに いった とき えいごで
せつめい しながら せいひんを しょうかい しました。
えいごが へたな ので、とても たいへん でした。

スミス: さいきん しゅっちょう しましたか。

もりた: いいえ。しばらく して いません。でも ちかい うちに
アメリカへ いくと ききました。

スミス: えいごを べんきょう して いるの ですか。

もりた: はい。じつは しごとの あとで えいかいわ きょうしつが
あります。

スミス: はたらきながら えいごを べんきょう するのは たいへん でしょうね。

もりた: ええ。すこし たいへん です。

スミス: じゃ, がんばって ください。

もりた: はい, ありがとう ございます。

II

A: すみませんが、しつもんが あります。いまは つごうが わるい ですか。

B: いいえ おんがくを ききながら インターネットを つかって いる だけ です。

A: これを せつめい して ほしいの ですが。わたしの せんせいが
「きょうじゅうに これを おえなさい」と いいました。いい ですか。

B: もちろん。

I

Sumisu: *Morita-san-wa bōeki gaisha-ni tsutomete iru-to kikimashita.*

Morita: *Sō desu. Iroirona mono-o yushutsu shite*

I

Smith: I heard you work for a trading company, Mr. Morita.

Morita: That's right. We export various products.

imasu. Yōroppa-ya Amerika-ni takusan yushutsu shite imasu.

We export a lot to Europe and America.

S: Hoka-no kuni-e yoku shucchō shimasu-ka.

S: Do you often travel to other countries?

M: Ē. Kyonen Doitsu-e ikimashita.

M: Yes, last year I went to Germany.

S: Dono kurai taizai shita-no desu-ka.

S: How long were you there?

M: Sanshūkan desu. Doitsu-ni itta toki eigo-de setsumei shinagara seihin-o shōkai shimashita. Eigo-ga heta-na node, totemo taihen deshita.

M: For three weeks. When I was in Germany, I explained things in English while I showed products. Because my English is terrible, it was very tough.

S: Saikin shucchō shimashita-ka.

S: Have you recently been on a trip?

M: Iie, shibaraku shite imasen, demo chikai uchi-ni Amerika-e iku-to kikimashita.

M: No, I have not for a long time, but I heard that I will go to America in the near future.

S: Eigo-o benkyō shite iru-no desu-ka.

S: Are you studying English?

M: Hai, jitsu-wa shigoto-no ato de eikaiwa kyōshitsu-ga arimasu.

M: Yes, actually I have an English conversation class after work.

S: Hatarakinagara Eigo-o benkyō suru-no-wa taihen deshō, ne.

S: Working while studing English must be very difficult.

M: Ē, sukoshi taihen desu.

M: Yes, it is a little difficult.

Quotes
Quotation marks are written differently in Japanese than in English. At the beginning of a quote, 「 is used. At the end of a quote, 」 is used.

-Shite hoshii
To state that you want another person to do something, use the -shite kudasai form learned before or -shite hoshii desu. ex. Kaita hon-o **misete hoshii desu**. I want you to show me the book you wrote. Exercises for this grammar pattern will be in Lesson 19.

ato de
after

bōeki gaisha
trading
company

bōeki suru
to trade

chikai uchi-ni
in the near
future

dame
not good

Doitsu
Germany

Eikaiwa
English
conversation

ganbaru(-u)
to do one's
best

hataraku(-u)
to work

heta(na)
poor at

intānetto
Internet

itsu made
until when

kuni
country

kyōjū-ni
by the end of
today

kyonen
last year

S: *Jā, ganbatte kudasai.*

M: *Hai, arigatō
gozaimasu.*

II

A: *Sumimasen-ga,
shitsumon-ga arimasu.
Ima-wa tsugō-ga warui
desu-ka.*

B: *Iie, ongaku-o kikinagara
intānetto-o tsukatte iru
dake desu.*

A: *Kore-o setsumei shite
hoshii-no desu ga.
Watashi-no sensei-
ga「kyōjū-ni kore-o
oenasai」-to iimashita.
Ii desu-ka.*

B: *Mochiron.*

S: Well, do your best.

M: Thank you.

II

A: Excuse me, I have
a question. Is now a
bad time?

B: No, I am only listening
to music and (while)
using the Internet.

A: I would like you to
explain this to me. My
teacher said, "Finish
this by the end of the
day." Is it alright?

B: Of course.

GRAMMAR EXPLANATION

1. Toki

To state "when I was a child," or "when I was
(something)," the grammar structure is as follows:

subject-**wa** + <u>noun-**no**</u> or <u>verb phrase</u> + **toki**

ex. ***Watashi-wa gakusei-no toki** takusan
benkyō shimashita.*
When I was a student, I studied a lot.

Watashi-wa kodomo-no toki, iroirona
hon-o yomimashita.
When I was a child, I read various books.

Sumisu-san-wa Nihon-ni itta toki,
kamera-o motte ikimashita.
When Mr. Smith went to Japan, he took a
camera.

Tanaka-san-wa daigaku-ni ita toki,
hotondo-no supōtsu-o shimashita.
When Miss Tanaka was in college, she
played almost all of the sports.

Hara-san-wa hirugohan-o taberu toki,
taitei resutoran-ni ikimasu.
When Mr. Hara eats lunch, he usually
goes to a restaurant.

2. -Nagara

To state that one is doing two things at the same
time, like eating while watching TV, or listening to
music while studying, use this pattern:

verb+*nagara*   main object   main verb

When using the *nagara* pattern, the verb that is
the easiest to do, or the one that is routine, is
paired with *nagara*. The action that is unusual or
special comes last. If both are equal, it does not
matter which is used with *nagara*.

ex. iyahōn-o **shinagara** jogingu shite imasu
using (lit. doing) earphones while jogging

Ganbatte Kudasai In English, when someone is faced with a difficult task, we usually say "good luck." The closest phrase to that in Japanese is *ganbatte kudasai,* which literally means "do your best."

131

mina-san
all of you

minna
everyone

miseru(-ru)
to show

mochiron
of course

omoi(i)
heavy

ryokō suru
to travel

saikin
recently

seihin
products

**setsumei
suru**
to explain

shibaraku
for a long
time

shitsumon
question

shōkai suru
to show,
recommend

**shucchō
suru**
to take a
business trip

sū(-u)
to inhale

tabako
cigarettes

*Sumisu-san-wa kōhī-o nominagara
shinbun-o yonde imasu.*
Mr. Smith drinks coffee while reading the
newspaper.

*Sumisu-san-wa o-kashi-o tabenagara
terebi-o mite imasu.*
Mr. Smith eats snacks while watching TV.

To form this pattern, drop *masu* and add *nagara*.

*ex. benkyō shimasu
benkyō shinagara*

mimasu
minagara

tabemasu
tabenagara

3. -To iimasu

When quoting someone, or expressing what
a person said, use the same grammar pattern
as for *-to omoimasu*, but substitute *-to iimasu*.
If using quotes, you must say exactly what the
person said. If not, you do not have to say the
exact words, but still use *-to iimashita*.

ex. Kare-wa Nihonjin da-to omoimasu.
I think he is Japanese.

Kare-wa 「Nihonjin da 」-to iimashita.
He said he is Japanese.

*Mitsumura-san-wa 「watashi-no kaisha-wa
kamera-o yushutsu suru 」-to iimashita.*

Mrs. Mitsumura said, "My company exports cameras."

Additionally, when stating that someone asked a question, use *-ka-to kikimashita*.

ex. *Sumisu-san-wa* ⌜*bōeki gaisha-ni tsutomete iru-**ka**⌟ **-to kikimashita**.*
Mr. Smith asked, "Do you work for a trading company?"

Mitsutake-san-wa ⌜*sono hon-ga omoi-**ka**⌟ **-to kikimashita**.*
Mrs. Mitsutake asked "Is that book heavy?"

Kikimasu also means hear:

ex. *Watashi-wa Matsumoto-san-ga kyō Kyōto-ni iku-**to kikimashita**.*
I heard that Mr. Matsumoto will go to Kyoto today.

4. Phrases

Another way to create noun phrases is to use:

(Noun-***no/ga***), (place or time), plain verb, object

ex. *Watashi-wa uchi-de hon-o yomimashita.*
I read a book at home.
***Watashi-no uchi-de yonda hon**-wa hōritsu-no hon deshita.*
The book I read at home was a law book.
chūgakkō-de Eigo-o benkyō shimashita
studied English at middle school

taizai
stay for a
period of time

tazuneru(-ru)
to visit

*tsugō-ga
warui*
a bad time

warui(i)
bad

ya
etc.

yoku
often

Yōroppa
Europe

yunyū suru
import

*yushutsu
suru*
export

Chūgakkō-de benkyō shita Eigo-wa
kantan deshita.
The English studied at middle school was simple.

Watashitachi-wa yūbe eiga-o mimashita.
We saw a movie last night.
Watashitachi-ga yūbe mita eiga-wa
totemo yokatta desu.
The movie we saw last night was very good.

Watashi-wa kuruma-o unten shimashita.
I drove a car.
Watashi-no unten shita kuruma-wa
Toyota-no kuruma deshita.
The car I drove was a Toyota.

Yamada-san-wa hon-o kakimashita.
Mrs. Yamada wrote a book.
Watashi-wa **Yamada-san-ga kaita hon**-
ga suki desu.
I like the book that Mrs. Yamada wrote.

EXERCISES
1. -Toki

Substitute the following phrases into this sentence:

ex. *Yōroppa-ni iku*

➡ *Sumisu-san-wa* **Yōroppa-ni itta** *toki,
iroirona hito-ni aimashita.*

Tōkyō-ni kuru
Ōsutoraria-o ryokō suru
daigaku-ni hairu
toshokan-ni tsutomete iru

2. -Nagara

Combine the following phrases using -*nagara*:

ex. *tabako-o sū, shinbun-o yomu*

➡ *tabako-o suinagara shinbun-o yonde imasu.*

iyahōn-o suru, jogingu suru
suwaru, denwa-o kakeru
rajio-o kiku, kuruma-o unten suru
Eigo-o benkyō suru, hataraku
terebi-o miru, gohan-o taberu
hon-o yomu, o-kashi-o taberu

3. -To iimasu, -to kikimasu

Place the sentences into the -*to iimasu* phrase:

ex. *Konban eiga-o mitai desu.*

➡ *Tanaka-san-wa「__konban eiga-o mitai__」-to iimashita.*

Kaisha-wa iroirona seihin-o yunyū shite imasu.
Hara-san-wa bōeki gaisha-ni tsutomete imasu.
Uchi-de tsukutta karei-wa karakatta desu.
Senshū katta tsukue-wa omokatta desu.
Tabako-o sū-no-wa dame desu.
Amerika-ni itta koto-ga arimasu.

ex. *Sumisu-san-wa Nihongo-ga wakarimasu-ka.*

➡ *Tanaka-san-wa「__Sumisu-san-wa Nihongo-ga wakaru-ka__」-to kikimashita.*

Mōri-san-wa ginkō-ni tsutometa koto-ga arimasu-ka.

Tazuneru is preceded by *o. ex. Yamori-san-wa Doitsu-o __tazunemashita__.* Mrs. Yamori visited Germany.

Ya
Ya can be used in place of *to* (and) to mean etc. Only one *ya* is needed, and if you use *ya*, you do not need *to* (unless *to* is being used to mean "with"). It usually comes after the first noun when listing objects or things. ex. *Ryokō suru toki kamera-__ya__, okane, chizu-o motte ikimasu.* When I travel I take a camera, money, a map, etc.

135

Hara-san-ga yomitagatte ita hon-wa sore deshita-ka.

Buraun-san-no tabetagatte ita shokuji-wa kore desu-ka.

Harada-san-no oku-san-ga tsukutta sushi-o tabeta koto-ga arimasu-ka.

Yūbe mita eiga-wa omoshirokatta desu-ka.

4. Phrases

Change the given sentences into noun phrases:

ex. Ōsutoraria-de tomodachi-ni aimashita.

➡ *Ōsutoraria-de atta tomodachi*

Baiten-de kippu-o kaimashita.
Sūpāmāketto-de ringo-o kaimashita.
Eigakan-de eiga-o mimashita.
Kissaten-de ocha-o nomimashita.
Tanaka-san-no uchi-de sakana-o tabemashita.

ex. Watashi-wa ocha-o iremashita.

➡ *Watashi-no ireta ocha*
➡ *Watashi-ga ireta ocha*

Hara-san-wa karei-o tsukurimashita.
Oku-san-wa tegami-o kakimashita.
Watashi-wa sake-o nomimashita.
Hanabusa-san-wa pātī-ni ikimashita.
Watashi-wa daigaku-de Nihongo-o naraimashita.
Ano hito-wa asoko-de hon-o yomimasu.

SHORT DIALOGUES

1. *ex.* ocha-o nomu, terebi-o miru, kissaten

   Azusa:Michiko-san-wa nani-o shite iru-no desu-ka.
   *Emiko: Michiko-san-wa **ocha-o nominagara terebi-o mite** imasu.*
   Azusa: Kanojo-wa mise-ni ikitagatte imasu-ka.
   *Emiko: Iie, 「**kissaten**-ni ikitai」-to iimashita.*

   1. ringo-o taberu, rajio-o kiku, resutoran-ni iku
   2. jūsu-o nomu, zasshi-o yomu, ginkō
   3. tabako-o sū, denwa-o kakeru, kusuriya
   4. niku-o taberu, terebi-o miru, biyōin
   5. isu-ni suwaru, bideo-o miru, kissaten

2. *ex.* daigaku-ni iru, Eigo

   *Hirakawa: **Daigaku-ni ita** toki, nani-o benkyō shimashita-ka.*
   *Nishiyama: **Daigaku-ni ita** toki, **Eigo**-o benkyō shimashita.*
   *H: Sō desu-ka. **Eigo**-o benkyō shinagara supōtsu-mo shimashita-ka.*
   N: Hai, shimashita.
   H: Taihen deshita, ne.

   1. kodomo-no, Eigo
   2. Amerika-ni iru, bungaku
   3. kōkō-ni iru, kagaku
   4. shōgakkō-ni iru, rekishi
   5. Yōroppa-ni sunde iru, Supeingo

De
To say that someone speaks in English, writes in *Hiragana*, etc., use *de*. *ex. Eigo-de hanashite kudasai.* Please say it in English. *Kanji-de kakimashita.* I wrote in *kanji*.

3. *ex.* Uchi-de bideo-o miru, omoshiroi

A: *Yūbe shigoto-no ato de nani-o shimashita-ka.*
B: **Uchi-de bideo-o mimashita.**
A: **Uchi-de mita bideo**-*wa* **omoshirokatta**
   desu-ka.
B: *Ē,* **omoshirokatta** *desu.*

1. resutoran-de shokuji-o suru, oishii
2. gakkō-de Supeingo-o benkyō suru,
   muzukashii
3. gekijō-de geki-o miru, yoi
4. mise-de ningyō-o kau, takai

SELF TEST
Unscramble the following sentences:
1. daigaku shimashita ni ita toki rekishi benkyō o.
2. de Tanaka-san iimashita wa no ato sake o nomitai
   to shigoto.
3. ano jogingu o shinagara iyahōn shite hito wa o
   imasu.
4. nai zenzen iimashita wa zasshi ga to Yamada-san.
5. tachinagara shite Hara-san wa hanashi-o imasu.

Fill in the blanks with *wa, ga, de, o, ni, to, no, ka, ne,* or X:
6. Toyota ___ tsutomete ita ___ toki ___ iroirona seihin
   _____ shōkai shimashita.
7. Harada-san ___ 「anata ___ kono hon ___ yonda
   ___」 ___ kikimashita.
8. Yamada-san ___ tsukutta ___ gohan ___ totemo
   ___ oishikatta desu.
9. Watashitachi ___ kinō ___ mita bideo ___
   sugokatta-n desu, ___.
10. Hara-san ___ 「anata ___ katta sētā ___ kirei da」
    ___ iimashita.

LESSON SIXTEEN
TABERAREMASU-KA

In this lesson you will learn:

- The potential form of verbs

- The -koto-ga dekiru expression

- The -ku naru and -ni naru phrases

DIALOGUE

I

A: いやな てんき ですね。

B: ほんとうに そう ですね。きょうは さむくて あめが ふって
   いますが あしたは てんきに なりますよ。

A: おちゃ でも のみましょうか。

B: はい。どこに いきましょうか。

A: ちかくに きっさてんが ありますよ。

B: そこで ケーキも たべられますか。

A: ええ。ケーキも おいて ありますよ。

II ひらかわさんの むすめの けっこん しき

A: ジョンソンさん こちらは ひらかわさん です。

ひらかわ: はじめまして よく いらっしゃいました。

ジョンソン: どうぞ よろしく。おめに かかれて こうえい です。
   きょうの けっこん しきは すばらしかった ですね。にほんの
   けっこん しきに でたのは これが はじめて です。

ひらかわ: ほんとう ですか。にほんごが じょうずに
   はなせますね。はつおんが とても いい です。

ジョンソン: いいえ。そんな ことは ありませんよ。

ひらかわ: どこで にほんごを べんきょう しましたか。

ジョンソン: はじめは ひとりで べんきょう しましたが, それ から
   にほんに きて にほんごの がっこうで べんきょう しました。

ひらかわ: もじは かけますか。

ジョンソン: はい。ひらがなと かたかなは かけますが、かんじは
   ぜんぜん しりません。

ひらかわ: ああ。かんじは にほんじん でも むずかしい ですよ。

I

A: *Iyana tenki desu, ne.*

B: *Hontō-ni sō desu ne. Kyō-wa samukute ame-ga futte imasu ga, ashita-wa tenki-ni narimasu, yo.*

I

A: The weather is unpleasant today, isn't it.

B: It really is. It is cold and rainy today, but tomorrow it will get better.

A: *Ocha demo nomimashō-ka.*

B: *Hai. Doko-ni ikimashō-ka.*

A: *Chikaku-ni kissaten-ga arimasu, yo.*

B: *Soko-de kēki-mo taberaremasu-ka.*

A: *Ē. Kēki-mo oite arimasu, yo.*

II Hirakawa-san-no musume-no kekkon shiki

A: *Jonson-san, kochira-wa Hirakawa-san desu.*

Hirakawa: *Hajimemashite, yoku irrashaimashita.*

Jonson: *Dōzo yoroshiku. Ome-ni kakarete kōei desu. Kyō-no kekkon shiki-wa subarashikatta desu, ne. Nihon-no kekkon shiki-ni deta-no-wa kore-ga hajimete desu.*

H: *Hontō desu-ka. Nihongo-ga jōzu-ni hanasemasu, ne. Hatsuon-ga totemo ii desu.*

J: *Iie, sonna koto-wa arimasen, yo.*

H: *Doko-de Nihongo-o benkyō shimashita-ka.*

J: *Hajime-wa hitori-de*

A: Shall we drink some (thing such as) tea?

B: Yes. Where shall we go?

A: There is a cafe nearby.

B: Can we also eat cake there?

A: Yes, they have (display) cake there.

II At Mrs. Hirakawa's daughter's wedding

A: Ms. Johnson, this is Mrs. Hirakawa.

Hirakawa: Nice to meet you; welcome.

Johnson: It is a pleasure to meet you. Today's wedding ceremony was wonderful, wasn't it. This is the first time I have been to a Japanese wedding.

H: Really. You can speak Japanese very well. Your pronunciation is very good.

J: No, not really.

H: Where did you study Japanese?

J: At first, I studied by

Greetings
In addition to the greetings learned previously, one can greet a Japanese person by saying that the weather is nice, or unpleasant. *Ii o-tenki desu, ne.* The weather's nice, isn't it? *Iyana o-tenki desu, ne.* The weather is unpleasant, isn't it?

Natsu yasumi
Yasumi means "holiday," or "rest time." When it is combined with a season, it means that season's vacation or holiday. *ex. natsu yasumi*, summer vacation; *fuyu yasumi*, winter vacation; *haru yasumi*, spring vacation. When combined with *hiru* to form *hiru yasumi*, it means "lunch time" at a school or office.

aki
autumn

asatte
the day after
tomorrow

atatakai(i)
warm

(o)bentō
box lunch

bukka
commodity
price(s)

chikaku
close, near

demo
such as, even
for

deru(-ru)
to attend

fuyu
winter

gaikoku
foreign
(country)

gakuhi
school tuition

hajime
at first

hare
clear

haru
spring

hatsuon
pronunciation

benkyō shimashita ga,
sore kara Nihon-ni kite
Nihongo-no gakkō-de
benkyō shimashita.

H: Moji-wa kakemasu-ka.

J: Hai. Hiragana-to kata-
kana-wa kakemasu
ga, kan-ji-wa zenzen
shirimasen.

H: Ā, kanji-wa Nihonjin
demo muzukashii
desu, yo.

myself, but then I
came to Japan and
studied at a Japanese
language school.

H: Can you write
Japanese letters?

J: Yes, I can write
in hiragana and
katakana, but I don't
know any kanji at all.

H: Oh, kanji is difficult
even for Japanese
people.

GRAMMAR EXPLANATION
1. Potential Form of Verbs (I can _____)

For -ru verbs, replace ru with rareru.

ex. ageru   age(ra)reru
miru   mi(ra)reru, (mieru)
kaeru   kae(ra)reru

For -u verbs, replace the final u with eru (tsu with teru).

ex. hanasu   hanaseru
kaku   kakeru
iku   ikeru
uru   ureru
motsu   moteru
matsu   materu

Exceptions: kuru   ko(ra)reru
iu   ieru

No potential form of *suru* exists, instead use *dekiru*.

To conjugate these verbs into the plain negative form, drop the final *ru* and add *nai*.

ex. *mi(ra)reru*   *mi(ra)renai, (mienai)*
    ikeru   *ikenai*

To change these verbs into the *masu* form, drop the final *ru* and add *masu*.

ex. *age(ra)reru*   *age(ra)remasu*
    kae(ra)reru   *kae(ra)remasu*

2. Koto-ga dekimasu

Another way to express potential verbs is the *koto-ga dekimasu* form. This phrase formation is similar to *koto-ga arimasu*.

<u>Subject</u>-***wa*** <u>noun</u>-***o*** <u>plain verb</u>+***koto-ga dekimasu***.

ex. *Tanaka-san-wa tenisu-o suru **koto-ga dekimasu**-ka.*
Mrs. Tanaka, can you play tennis?

*Sumisu-san-wa hitori-de moji-o kaku **koto-ga dekimasu**-ka.*
Mr. Smith, can you write Japanese letters by yourself?

To answer: *Hai, dekimasu.*
           Iie, dekimasen.

As the Japanese language changes, people sometimes drop the middle *ra* from potential *-ru* verbs. ex. *kaereru* instead of *kaerareru*

Miru
The potential of *miru* is sometimes *mieru*, sometimes *mirareru*. *Mieru* means that one can see an object easily, whereas *mirareru* means that one can see an object that is not in plain sight.

<table>
<tr><td>

hitori-de
by oneself,
alone

iya(na)
unpleasant

jibun-de
by oneself

jōzu(na)
skillful

kaisei
very nice
weather

kasa
umbrella

kēki
cake

kekkon shiki
wedding
ceremony

kekkon suru
to marry

kumori
cloudy

moji
Japanese
letters

natsu
summer

-nin
counter for
people

niwa
garden

</td><td>

3. -Ku narimasu, ni narimasu

To state that "It is becoming cold," "It is getting better," or "I am (becoming) late," etc., for *i* adjectives, drop the final *i* and add *ku naru.*

ex. *ōkii*
   ōkiku narimasu
   becomes big
   Kodomo-wa ōkiku natte imasu.
   The child is becoming bigger.

   Soto-wa samuku narimashita.
   It became cold outside.

For *na* adjectives, drop the final *na,* and add *ni naru.*

ex. *Kare-wa Nihongo-ga jōzu-ni natte imasu.*
   He is getting better (skillful) at Japanese.

   Niwa-ga kirei-ni narimashita.
   The garden became beautiful.

EXERCISES
1. Potential verbs
Substitute the given verbs into the sentences:

ex. *koko-de matsu*
   A: *Sumisu-san-wa **koko-de matemasu**-ka?*
   B: *Hai, matemasu.*
      Iie, matemasen.

   kekkon shiki-ni deru   rokuji-ni okiru
   kissaten-ni hairu   gaikoku-ni iku
   ima kara uchi-ni kaeru
   jibun-de densha-ni noru

</td></tr>
</table>

144

2. -O + verb, -ga + potential verb

Change the following phrases as shown:

> *ex. rajio-o kiku*
>
> ➡ *rajio-ga kikemasu*

> | | |
> |---|---|
> | *sake-o nomu* | *Eigo-o oshieru* |
> | *Nihongo-o hanasu* | *sushi-o taberu* |
> | *ocha-o ireru* | *kuruma-o kau* |
> | *kasa-o kau* | *moji-o yomu* |
> | *kyūka-o toru* | *kippu-o sagasu* |
> | *yakyū-o suru* | *shashin-o toru* |
> | *jisho-o tsukau* | *o-bentō-o taberu* |
> | *kuruma-o unten suru* | |
> | *shakaigaku-o benkyō suru* | |

O and ga
As learned previously, objects are followed by *o* in a sentence. However, when the verb is changed into its potential form, change the *o* to *ga*. *ex. Eigo-**o** hanashimasu.* I speak English. *Eigo-**ga** hanasemasu.* I can speak English.

3. Negative potential verbs

Place the phrases and negative potential verbs into the following sentence:

> *ex. oku-san-no hoshigatte iru kuruma, kaenai*
>
> ➡ *Yamada-san-wa **oku-san-no hoshigatte iru kuruma**-ga **kaemasen**.*

> *kodomo-ga kaita kanji, yomenai*
>
> *shujin-no tsukutta sushi, taberarenai*
>
> *kodomo-no hairitagatte iru daigaku-no gakuhi, haraenai*
>
> *kodomo-ga hoshigatte ita omocha-no namae, oboerarenai*

oboeru(-ru)
to remember, memorize

oku(-u)
to display, put out for sale

ome-ni kakarete kōei desu
very pleased to meet you (polite)

omocha
toy

renshū suru
to practice

-sama
polite form of -san

subarashii(i)
great, wonderful

tashika(na)
certain, sure

tenisu
tennis

tenki
weather, nice weather

watakushi
I (formal)

4. Koto-ga dekiru

Place the given phrases into the *koto-ga dekimasu* phrase:

ex. sushi-o tsukuru

> A: **Sushi-o tsukuru** *koto-ga dekimasu-ka.*
> B: *Ē, dekiru-to omoimasu.*

> *Nihongo-de bōeki-o setsumei suru*
> *Nihon-no chizu-o yomu*
> *Tanaka-san-no tanjōbi-no pātī-ni iku*
> *geki-no kippu-o kau*
> *Supeingo-o hanasu*
> *kanji-o yomu*

5. -Ku narimasu, -ni narimasu

Match the following phrases:

1. *Kono goro-wa hon-ga*   a.*takaku narimashita.*
2. *Akachan-wa*   b.*waruku narimasu.*
3. *Hara-san-wa Eigo-ga*   c.*osoku narimashita.*
4. *Asatte tenki-ga*   d.*ōkiku natte imasu.*
5. *Sumimasen,*   e.*jōzu-ni natte imasu.*

6. Memorize the counters for people:

1 person *hitori*	7 people *shichi/nana-nin*
2 people *futari*	8 people *hachi-nin*
3 people *san-nin*	9 people *kyū-nin*
4 people *yo-nin*	10 people *jū-nin*
5 people *go-nin*	11 people *jūichi-nin*
6 people *roku-nin*	12 people *jūni-nin*

The pattern continues regularly, number + *nin*

SHORT DIALOGUES

1. *ex.* koko-ni kuru, san-nin

   Satoshi: *Kyō-wa ii o-tenki desu, ne.*
   Takashi: *Sō desu ne. Kaisei desu, ne.*
   Satoshi: *Nan-nin **koko-ni kimasu**-ka.*
   Takashi: ***San-nin koko-ni kuru**-to omoimasu.*

   1. jogingu-o suru, futari-de
   2. kekkon shiki-ni deru, hyaku-nin-de
   3. shashin-o toru, hitori-de
   4. yakyū-no geimu-o suru, jūni-nin-de

2. *ex.* sukī, dekiru, suru, iku

   Sumisu: *Anata-wa **sukī**-ga **dekimasu**-ka.*
   Imai: *Ē, watashi-wa sukoshi **sukī**-ga **dekiru**-to omoimasu.*
   Sumisu: *Subarashii desu, ne.*
   Imai: *Demo, jōzu-ni **dekimasen**.*
   Sumisu: *Boku-wa zenzen **sukī**-ga **dekimasen**. **Sukī-o suru**-no-wa muzukashii desu-ka.*
   Imai: *Sukoshi muzukashii-to omoimasu. Jā, kondo issho-ni **ikimashō***
   Sumisu: *Watashi-ni oshieraremasu-ka.*
   Imai: *Mochiron.*
   Sumisu: *Arigatō.*

   1. tenpura, tsukuru, tsukuru
   2. kanji, kaku, benkyō suru
   3. tenisu, dekiru, iku
   4. moji, yomu, benkyō suru
   5. kuruma, unten dekiru, renshū suru

People+de
When stating that one person does something, or a number of people do something together, use *de*. *Hitori-de unten shite imasu.* One person is driving. *San-nin-de ikimashita.* Three people went.

3. *ex.* fuyu, sukī-o dekiru, atatakai

Urabe: **Fuyu** yasumi Tanaka-san-wa
sukī-o suru koto-ga dekimasu-ka.
Tanaka: **Atatakaku** natta kara dekimasen.
Urabe: Zannen desu, ne.
Tanaka: Daijōbu desu. Kyōto-ni ikimasu.
Asoko-de iroirona koto-ga dekimasu.
Urabe: Sore-wa ii desu, ne.

1. natsu, oyogu, samui
2. fuyu, Hokkaido-ni iku, tenki-ga warui
3. haru, sakkā-o suru, samui
4. aki, tenisu-o suru, samui

SELF-TEST
Translate the following sentences into Japanese:

1. That baby can walk by herself!

2. Grandmother can speak English.

3. Mrs. Hara can play tennis.

4. The weather is becoming cold.

5. Four people can sit down.

Unscramble the following sentences:

6. wa iku natsu watashi dekimasu ga Sapporo koto yasumi ni

7. Tanaka imasu wa ni sukī jōzu natte ga san

8. ni koraremasu de ka uchi hitori.

9. shiki omoimasu subarashikatta to wa kekkon

10. de wa desu o-bentō o tabeta futari gakkō no

LESSON SEVENTEEN
YOMITAKU NAI

In this lesson you will learn:

- Stating what you do not want to do

- Plain past negative verbs

- How to state your plans

- Numbers above ten thousand

DIALOGUE

I

あや: こうすけくん ゆうべ えいご べんきょう したの。
こうすけ: いや べんきょう しなかった。
あや: どうして あなたは べんきょう しなかったの。
こうすけ: じかんが なかった。あやちゃんは。
あや: すこし べんきょう したよ。この ほんも よんだの。
こうすけ: ぼくは よまなかったよ。
あや: これ から よみたい。
こうすけ: いや よみたくない。

II

A: この しゅうまつは よていが ありますか。
B: ええ。ともだちが アメリカから たずねて きます。くうこうへ
　 かれを むかえに いきます。
A: おともだちは ホテルに とまるの ですか。
B: いいえ。にほんごが はなせない ので、ホテルには
　 とまりたくないと いって いました。
A: ところで かりた ビデオ を いつ かえしましょうか。
B: あしたで いい ですよ。わたしは でかけて いますが、わたしの
　 おとうとに わたして ください。たのしかった ですか。
A: ええ。とても すばらしかった です。
B: また いつでも どうぞ。

I

Aya: *Kōsuke-kun, yūbe Eigo-o benkyō shita-no.*

Kōsuke: *Iya, benkyō shinakatta.*

A: *Dōshite anata-wa benkyō shinakatta-no.*

K: *Jikan-ga nakatta. Aya-chan-wa.*

I

Aya: Kosuke, did you study English last night?

Kosuke: No, I didn't.

A: Why didn't you study?

K: I didn't have time. How about you?

A: *Sukoshi benkyō shita yo. Kono hon-mo yonda-no.*

A: I studied a little. Did you read this book already?

K: *Boku-wa yomanakatta, yo.*

K: I did not read it.

A: *Kore kara yomitai.*

A: Do you want to read it?

K: *Iya, yomitaku nai.*

K: No, I don't want to read it.

II

II

A: *Kono shūmatsu-wa yotei-ga arimasu-ka.*

A: Do you have plans for this weekend?

B: *Ē. Tomodachi-ga Amerika-kara tazunete kimasu. Kūkō-e kare-o mukae-ni ikimasu.*

B: Yes, my friend is visiting from America. I will go pick him up at the airport.

A: *O-tomodachi-wa hoteru-ni tomaru-no desu-ka.*

A: Will your friend stay in a hotel?

B: *Iie, Nihongo-ga hanasenai node, hoteru-ni-wa tomaritaku nai-to itte imashita.*

B: No, he cannot speak Japanese, so he said he doesn't want to stay in a hotel.

A: *Tokorode, karita bideo-o itsu kaeshimashō-ka.*

A: By the way, when should I return the video you lent me?

B: *Ashita-de ii desu, yo. Watashi-wa dekakete imasu ga, watashi-no otōto-ni watashite kudasai. Tanoshikatta desu-ka.*

B: Tomorrow is fine. I will be out, but you can give it to my brother. Did you enjoy it?

A: *Ē. Totemo subarashikatta desu.*

A: Yes. It was wonderful.

B: *Mata itsudemo dōzo.*

B: (Borrow it) again anytime.

Irasshaimasu
Irasshaimasu is the polite word for *imasu*, *ikimasu*, and *kimasu*. When speaking to someone who is of a higher position than you, or someone you wish to show respect to, use *irasshaimasu* instead of *imasu*, *ikimasu*, or *kimasu. ex. Tanaka-san-wa ginkō-ni* **irasshaimashita-**ka. Mr. Tanaka, did you go to the bank? *Okā-san-wa* **irasshaimasu-**ka. Is your mother there?

-chan
used insted
of -san at the
end of small
children's and
girl's names

daibu
very

deru(-ru)
to leave

dōshite
why

heya
room

hikōki
airplane

hiku(-u)
to look up in a
dictionary

hora
here, look

irassharu(-u)
to go, come,
be (honorific)

iya
no (informal)

jā mata
see you later

kaesu(-u)
to return
something

GRAMMAR EXPLANATION

1. -Taku nai

As learned previously, to state that you want to do
something, change *masu* to *tai* and add *desu*. If
you do **not** want to do something, drop the *i desu*
and add *-ku arimasen*. For the plain form, use *nai*
instead of *arimasen*.

> *ex. Niku-o tabetai desu.*
> I want to eat meat.
>
> *Niku-o tabetaku arimasen.*
> I don't want to eat meat.
>
> *Iyahōn-o shitaku nai-to omoimasu.*
> I do not think I want to use earphones.

2. -Nakatta

To change a plain negative verb into past form,
drop the final *i* and add *nakatta*.

ex. *yamenai*	does not give up
yamenakatta	did not give up
wakaranai	does not understand
wakaranakatta	did not understand

For *i* adjectives, use the *ku* form and add *nakatta*.

> *ex. kowaku arimasen deshita*
> was not frightening
> *kowaku nakatta*
> was not frightening (plain)

*tanoshi**ku nakatta***
was not enjoyable

When using *desu*, or a *na* adjective, drop *dewa arimasen deshita* and add *ja nakatta*.

ex. *sensei dewa arimasen deshita*
was not a teacher

*sensei **ja nakatta***	was not a teacher
*jisho **ja nakatta***	was not a dictionary
*yūmei **ja nakatta***	was not famous

The plain past negative adjectives and verbs can modifiy nouns when directly preceding them.

ex. *Tēburu-wa ōkikunakatta.*
The table was not big.
*ōkiku**nakatta** tēburu*
the table that was not big

Kodomo-wa asobanakatta.
The child did not play.
*asoba**nakatta** kodomo*
the child that did not play

Deru
When *deru* is used to mean "to leave," *-o* precedes it, not *-ni*. ex. *Kare-wa shichiji-ni uchi-**o** demasu.* He leaves home at 7:00.

Hora
Hora is used when giving an object to someone. It is like saying, "Here you are."

kai
desu ka
(informal)

kariru(-ru)
to borrow

kasu(-u)
to lend, rent

katarogu
catalogue,
brochure

kimi
you (informal
- only men
use)

kiro
kilo

kowai(i)
frightening

kūkō
airport

(o)kyaku
visitor

mā mā
so-so

meshiagaru(-u)
to eat (polite)

mukae-ni iku
go to pick
someone up

Narita
airport near
Tokyo

3. Chigaimasu

To express that two things are different, use the
following sentence pattern:

Item one-*wa* item two-*to chigaimasu*.

> ex. *Nihon-wa Amerika-to zuibun chigaimasu.*
> Japan is very different from America.
>
> *Kore-wa Emiko-san-no sunde ita apāto-*
> *to chigaimasu.*
> This is different from Emiko's apartment,
> or this is not Emiko's apartment.

4. Yotei desu

To state that you have plans to do something, use
a plain verb + *yotei desu*.

> ex. *Okurimono-o kau yotei desu.*
> I plan to buy a present.
>
> *Yamada-san-ni katarogu-o miseru yotei*
> *deshita.*
> I planned to show the catalogue to Mr.
> Yamada.

Use *yotei* when talking about your future plans
so that you do not appear presumptuous.

EXERCISES

1. -Taku arimasen

Conjugate the following verbs to the -*taku arimasen* form:

ex. rekishi-o benkyō suru

Shu: Azusa-san-wa **rekishi-o benkyō shitai** desu-ka.

Azusa: *Iie,* **rekishi-o benkyō shitaku** *arimasen.*

toranpu-de asobu	*terebi-o miru*
ongaku-o kiku	*hikōki-ni noru*
zasshi-o yomu	*kūkō-ni iku*
kōhī-o ireru	*jisho-o kau*
kanji-o kaku	*tenisu-o suru*

2. Plain negative past

Change the following into plain negative past tense:

ex. sumāto fon dewa arimasen deshita
➡ *sumāto fon ja nakatta*

> *hikōki dewa arimasen deshita*
> *kyōju dewa arimasen deshita*
> *okurimono dewa arimasen deshita*
> *o-bentō dewa arimasen deshita*
> *gaikokujin dewa arimasen deshita*

Toothpicks
After eating sushi or sashimi in a Japanese restaurant, it is common for people to use toothpicks to clean their teeth. When you do this, place your free hand over your mouth. It is not polite to clean your teeth without covering your mouth.

okurimono
present

oru(-ru)
iru (humble)

ototoi
the day before
yesterday

rusu(-u)
to be out or
away from
home

shūmatsu
weekend

tanoshii(i)
enjoyable

tomaru(-u)
to come to
a stop, sleep
over

tsukeru(-ru)
to attach,
stick on

un
yes (informal)

watasu(-u)
to hand over,
deliver

yotei
plans,
schedule

zenbu
all

ex. oishiku arimasen deshita
➡ oishiku nakatta

sugoku arimasen deshita
ōkiku arimasen deshita
subarashiku arimasen deshita
atarashiku arimasen deshita
furuku arimasen deshita

ex. watasanai
➡ watasanakatta

shinai   misenai
tsukawanai   awanai
toranai

3. Plain negative past

Place the following phrases into the sentences
using the plain negative past tense form:

ex. Nobu-kun-wa kuru.
A: **Nobu-kun-wa kita**-no.
B: Iie, **Nobu-kun-wa konakatta**-to
omoimasu.

Shu-kun-wa matte iru.
Yuki-chan-wa shōgakkō-de Eigo-o
narau.
Hiroko-chan-wa neru.
Kare-wa shichiji-ni uchi-o deru.
Kyōto-de shashin-o toru.
Tomoe-chan-wa ongaku-o kikeru.

Jun-kun-wa chūgakkō-ni iku.
Satoshi-kun-wa ie-ni haireru.
Kinō ame-ga furu.
Takashi-kun-wa Eigo-ga wakaru.
Geki-no kippu-wa takai.
Shu-kun-ga hanashita Eigo-wa jōzu da.
Yūbe atta hito-wa kyōju da.

4. Memorize the following numbers:

10,000 *ichiman*   1,000,000,000 *jūoku*
100,000 *jūman*   10,000,000,000 *hyakuoku*
1,000,000 *hyakuman* 100,000,000,000 *senoku*
10,000,000 *senman*   1,000,000,000,000 *itchō*
100,000,000 *ichioku*

5. Say the following numbers:

ex. 2,941,008,357
➡ *nijū kyū oku, yonsen hyaku man,*
    hassen, sanbyaku gojūshichi

     1,000,892,000   329,000,227,451
     9,296,460   1,947,091,253,008
     2,169,292,845   45,728,134,978
     562,728,500

Orimasu
Orimasu, the humble word for *imasu*, should be used when referring to yourself or someone from your group when you are trying to show humility. ex. *Imōto-wa Amerika-ni sunde* **orimasu.** My younger sister lives in America. **Never** use *orimasu* to refer to someone that you are speaking to.

SHORT DIALOGUES

1. *ex.* san-nen, Kyōto-ni irassharu, iku

Sumisu: *Tanaka-sama-wa dochira-ni tsutomete irasshaimasu-ka.*
Tanaka: *Mitsubushi ginkō-ni tsutomete orimasu. Hara-san-wa ⌈Sumisu-sama-wa Toyota-ni tsutomete inagara Nihongo-mo benkyō shite irassharu⌋ -to itte imashita.*
Sumisu: *Sō desu.*
Tanaka: *Nihon-ni mō dono kurai irasshaimasu-ka.*
Sumisu: **San-nen** *gurai Nihon-ni sunde orimasu.*
Tanaka: *Sumisu-sama-wa* **Kyōto-ni irasshatta** *koto-ga arimasu-ka.*
Sumisu: *lie,* **Kyōto-ni itta** *koto-wa arimasen. Totemo* **ikitai***-to omoimasu.*

1. ichinen, Hokkaido-ni irassharu, iku
2. hachikagetsu, Ōsaka-ni irassharu, iku
3. ikkagetsu, sushi-o meshiagaru, taberu
4. rokkagetsu, tenpura meshiagaru, taberu

2. *ex.* resutoran-ni iku, sukoshi tsukarete iru

> *Tanaka:*   *Shigoto-no ato de kimi-wa* **resutoran-ni ikanai**-*kai.*
>
> *Sumisu:*   *Iya,* **Ikitaku** *nai, yo.* **Sukoshi tsukarete iru** *kara. Ashita-no hō-ga ii yo.*
>
> *Tanaka:*   *Un, wakatta. Katarogu-o mō yonda-kai.*
>
> *Sumisu:*   *Un, zenbu yonda, yo. Hora, koko da yo.*

    1. kissaten-ni iku, isogashii
    2. sake-o nomu, sukoshi tsukarete iru
    3. eiga-o miru, purojekuto-o shite iru
    4. jogingu-o suru, isogashii

3. *ex.* mise-ni itta, jikan, iku

> *Morita:*   *Ototoi* **mise-ni ikimashita**-*ka.*
>
> *Jonson:*   *Iie,* **mise-ni ikimasen deshita**.
>
> *Morita:*   *Dōshite* **ikanakatta**-*no desu-ka.*
>
> *Jonson:*   **Jikan**-*ga nakatta-no desu.*
>
> *Morita:*   *Zannen deshita ne.*
>
> *Jonson:*   *Sō desu ne. Demo, sugu-ni* **iku** *yotei desu kara.*

    1. sumāto fon-o katta, okane, kau
    2. resutoran-de tabeta, okane, taberu
    3. Hirakawa-san-to hanashita, jikan, hanasu
    4. jisho-o katta, okane, kau
    5. resutoran-de sake-o nonda, jikan, nomu

SELF-TEST

Translate the following sentences into Japanese:

1. I did not buy a present last night (plain).

2. Here you are.

3. I did not have enough time.

4. I think I do not want to go to the temple.

5. Do you work at Honda, Mr. Hara (honorific)?

6. This weekend I do not want to ski.

7. I am living in Tokyo (humble).

8. The airport was not large (plain form).

9. Japanese magazines and American magazines are different.

10. Tomorrow I plan to go to Australia.

LESSON EIGHTEEN
SENSEI-GA KUDASAIMASHITA

In this lesson you will learn:

- Receiving verbs

- Polite and humble family terms

- How to state ages

DIALOGUE

I

ジョンソン: はらださんの おたく ですか。

はらだ: はい、そう です。ああ ジョンソンさん どうぞ
あがって ください。

ジョンソン: おじゃま します。これ つまらない もの です けど。
めしあがって ください。

はらだ: どうも ありがとう ございます。いただきます。
ジョンソンさんは ごきょうだい いらっしゃいますか。

ジョンソン: はい。おとうとが おります。

はらだ: おとうとさんは おいくつ ですか。

ジョンソン: じゅうろくさい です。

はらだ: おとうとさんは にほんに いらっしゃった ことが
ありますか。

ジョンソン: まだ ありません。でも、おとうとは とても にほんに
きたがって います。すてきな かびん ですね。

はらだ: ありがとう ございます。これは けっこん いわいに
ともだち から いただいた もの です。

II

ジョンソン: ごちそうさま でした。

はらだ: もう いいの ですか。ビールを もっと いかが ですか。

ジョンソン: いいえ もう けっこう です。ありがとう ございました。

はらだ: おへやを あんない しましょう。ふとんで ねた ことが
ありますか。

ジョンソン: まだ ありません。ごしんせつ ありがとう ございます。

I

Jonson: *Harada-san-no o-taku desu-ka.*

Harada: *Hai, sō desu. Ā, Jonson-san dōzo agatte kudasai.*

I

Johnson: Is this the Harada residence?

Harada: Yes, that's correct. Oh, Mr. Johnson, please come in.

J: *Ojama shimasu. Kore tsumaranai mono desu kedo. Meshiagatte kudasai.*

J: I'm interrupting you. Here is a small gift. Please enjoy it (please eat).

H: *Dōmo arigatō gozaimasu. Itadakimasu. Jonson-san-wa go-kyōdai irasshaimasu-ka.*

H: Thank you very much. Mr. Johnson, do you have any brothers or sisters?

J: *Hai, otōto-ga orimasu.*

J: Yes, I have a younger brother.

H: *Otōto-san-wa o-ikutsu desu-ka.*

H: How old is your brother?

J: *Jūroku-sai desu.*

J: He's sixteen years old.

H: *Otōto-san-wa Nihon-ni irasshatta koto-ga arimasu-ka.*

H: Has he ever been to Japan?

J: *Mada arimasen. Demo, otōto-wa totemo Nihon-ni kitagatte imasu. Sutekina kabin desu, ne.*

J: Not yet. However, he really wants to come to Japan. That is a gorgeous vase.

H: *Arigatō gozaimasu. Kore-wa kekkon iwai-ni tomodachi-kara itadaita mono desu.*

H: Thank you. It was a wedding gift from a friend.

II

J: *Gochisō-sama deshita.*

J: It was a feast!

H: *Mō ii-no desu-ka. Bīru-o motto ikaga desu-ka.*

H: Would you like more? Would you like more beer?

J: *Iie, mō kekkō desu. Arigatō gozaimashita.*

J: No, I'm fine. Thank you very much.

Tsumaranai mono
Tsumaranai mono desu kedo, dōzo, is a common expression when giving someone a small gift. It literally means "this is junk, but please accept it," and it is a humble form of asking someone to accept your gift. Whenever you are invited to a Japanese home, it is polite to bring a small gift to express appreciation for their hospitality. A souvenir from your home country is a good idea.

163

annai suru
to take and
show

buchō
boss

futon
Japanese bed

genkin
cash

**gochisō-
sama deshita**
it was a feast,
thanks for the
meal

**iie, kekkō
desu**
no thank you

ikutsu
how old

itadakimasu
the word of
thanks uttered
before eating

itadaku(-u)
to receive

iwai
celebration

kabin
vase

kagi
key

kekkō(na)
fine

H: *O-heya-o annai
shimashō. Futon-de
neta koto-ga arimasu-ka.*

J: *Mada arimasen.
Go-shinsetsu arigatō
gozaimasu.*

H: I shall show you your
room. Have you ever
slept on a futon bed?

J: Not yet. Thank you for
your kindness.

GRAMMAR EXPLANATION

1. Receiving

Different words are used when talking about
giving and receiving, depending on the position of
both the giver and receiver.

kuremasu

To be given a gift from an **equal**. The giver is the
subject, receiver is the indirect object.

Giver-*ga* receiver-*ni* object-*o* **kuremasu**.

ex. *Tanaka-san-ga (watashi-ni) ningyō-o*
kuremashita.
Mrs. Tanaka gave me a Japanese doll.

*Tanjōbi-no iwai-ni imōto-ga watashi-
ni kono mōfu-o* ***kuremashita***.
For my birthday, my sister gave me
this blanket.

kudasaimasu

To be given a gift from a **superior.** The giver is the subject, receiver the indirect object.

> Giver-**ga** receiver-**ni** object-**o** **kudasaimasu**.

> ex. *Morita-sensei-ga watashi-ni jisho-o* **kudasaimashita.**
> My teacher, Mr. Morita, gave me a dictionary.

> *Sensei-ga Hara-san-ni hon-o kudasaimashita.*
> The teacher gave Mr. Hara a book.

moraimasu

To receive a gift from an **equal.** The receiver is the subject, giver the indirect object.

> Receiver-**wa** giver-**ni** object-**o** **moraimasu**.

> ex. *Watashi-wa haha-ni saifu-o* **moraimashita**.
> I received a wallet from my mother.

> *Tanaka-san-wa Sumisu-san-ni omiyage-o* **moraimashita**.
> Ms. Tanaka received a souvenir from Mr. Smith.

Noodles
You may be surprised the first time you eat noodles with Japanese people because they slurp them *loudly*. In fact, they may think you are not enjoying your noodles unless you slurp them as well!

konpyūtā
computer

kudasaru(-u)
to be given

kureru(-ru)
to be given

kyaku
visitor

makura
pillow

mōfu
blanket

morau(-u)
to receive

omiyage
souvenir

omiyageya
souvenir shop

otaku
residence

**rokku
konsāto**
rock concert

-sai
added to a
number to
indicate how
old someone
is

saifu
wallet

itadakimasu

To receive a gift from a **superior**. The receiver is
the subject, giver is the indirect object.

Receiver-**wa** giver-**ni** object-**o** *itadakimasu.*

ex. *Imai-san-wa Yamada-san-ni kabin-o*
itadakimashita.
Mrs. Imai received a vase from Mr.
Yamada.

Watashi-wa Hara-san-no okā-san-
ni rokku konsāto-no kippu-o
itadakimashita.
I received a rock concert ticket from
Miss Hara's mother.

To summarize:

Giver-**ga** receiver-**ni** object-**o** **kudasaimasu.**
kuremasu.

Receiver-**wa** giver-**ni** object-**o** *itadakimasu.*
moraimasu.

166

EXERCISES

1. Family terms

Memorize the following chart. Use polite words when referring to another's family, and humble terms when speaking of your own:

	Polite	**Humble**
Family	go-kazoku	kazoku
Mother	okā-san	haha
Father	otō-san	chichi
Parent	oyago-san	oya
Parents	go-ryōshin	ryōshin
Wife	oku-san	kanai/tsuma
Husband	go-shujin	shujin
Child	o-ko-sama	
	kodomo-san	kodomo
Son	musuko-san	musuko
	bottchan	
Daughter	musume-san	musuko
	ojō-san	
Sibling(s)	go-kyōdai	kyōdai
Older sister	onē-san	ane
Younger sister	imōto-san	imōto
Older brother	onii-san	ani
Younger brother	otōto-san	otōto
Aunt	oba-san	oba
Uncle	oji-san	oji
Cousin	o-itoko-san	itoko
Grandmother	obā-san	sobo
Grandfather	ojii-san	sofu

Agatte kudasai
Japanese people invite visitors to "step up" to their homes because there usually are one or two steps at the main entrances of most homes.

shikibuton
mattress

shikifu
sheet

shinsetsu(na)
kindness

suteki(na)
tasteful, looks sharp

taoru
towel

tatami
a reed mat covering the floor

teinei(na)
polite

tsumaranai mono
this small gift

yoku nemure-mashita
good night's sleep (lit. slept well)

zabuton
floor cushion

2. Family terms

Use each term to convey respect and humility:

ex. okā-san, haha

A: **Okā-san**-wa irasshaimasu-ka.

B: lie. **Haha**-wa orimasen.

otō-san, chichi	onii-san, ani
imōto-san, imōto	onē-san, ane
go-shujin, shujin	oku-san, kanai
otōto-san, otōto	

3. Giving and Receiving

Substitute the terms into the following sentences:

Subject-ga watashi-ni **object**-o kuremashita.

Subjects	Objects
haha	konpyūtā
ane	shatsu
Hirakawa-san	kagi
Mōri-san	mōfu

Watashi-wa **giver**-ni **object**-o moraimashita.

Givers	Objects
imōto	makura
Hanabusa-san	taoru
Kitamura-san	kippu
otōto	genkin

Subject-ga watashi-ni **object**-o kudasaimashita.

Subjects	Objects
Morita-sensei	jisho
Yamashita-san	okurimono

buchō	*hon*
sensei	*kaban*

Watashi-wa **giver***-ni* **object***-o itadakimashita.*

Givers	Objects
Yagi-san-no oku-san	*kutsu*
Tanaka-san	*megane*
Nishiyama-san	*taoru*
Hara-san-no okā-san	*kutsushita*

4. Counter for long, thin objects like pencils, bottles, etc:

1	*ippon*	6	*roppon*
2	*nihon*	7	*nanahon*
3	*sanbon*	8	*happon/hachihon*
4	*yonhon*	9	*kyūhon*
5	*gohon*	10	*juppon*

5. Ages:

1	*issai*	11	*jūissai*
2	*nisai*	12	*jūnisai*
3	*san-sai*	13	*jūsan-sai*
4	*yon-sai*	14	*jūyon-sai*
5	*go-sai*	15	*jūgo-sai*
6	*roku-sai*	16	*jūroku-sai*
7	*nana-sai*	17	*jūnana-sai*
8	*hassai*	18	*jūhassai*
9	*kyū-sai*	19	*jūkyū-sai*
10	*jussai*	20	*nijussai*

This pattern continues regularly. Change *jussai* to *sanjussai*, *yonjussai*, etc.

Souvenirs
In Japan, souvenirs include food from another country as well as small gifts.

Slippers
Whenever entering a Japanese house, always remove your shoes. Slippers can be found just inside the entrance. Be sure to remove your slippers when walking on a *tatami* mat. Also, there are often separate slippers used in the bathroom. You will find them just inside the bathroom door.

SHORT DIALOGUES

1. *ex.* ane, onē-san, jūhassai

Tanaka:	*Buraun-san, go-kyōdai-wa irasshaimasu-ka.*
Buran:	*Ē, **ane**-ga imasu.*
Tanaka:	***Onē-san**-wa Nihon-ni irasshatta koto-ga arimasu-ka.*
Buran:	*Iie, demo **ane**-wa hayaku Nihon-ni ikitai-to itte imashita.*
Tanaka:	*Sō desu-ka. **Onē-san**-wa o-ikutsu desu-ka.*
Buran:	***Jūhassai** desu.*

1. ani, onii-san, jūkyū-sai
2. otōto, otōto-san, nijūgo-sai
3. imōto, imōto-san, sanjūissai

2. *ex.* wanpīsu, chichi, yomitagatte ita hon

Morita:	*Sutekina **wanpīsu** desu ne. Nihon-de katta-no desu-ka.*
Sumisu:	*Iie, kore-wa kyonen **chichi**-ga kuremashita.*
Morita:	*Sō desu-ka. Tokorode, Anata-ga **yomitagatte ita hon**-o go-shujin-ni moraimashita-ka.*
Sumisu:	*Hai. Kinō shujin-ni moraimashita.*

1. tokei, haha, kaitagatte ita wanpīsu
2. sētā, Tanaka-san, mitagatte ita bideo
3. bōshi, imōto, kaitagatte ita kasa
4. kabin, Yamada-san, hoshigatte ita zabuton

3. *ex.* nekutai, Hanabusa-san, Kitamura-san-no okā-san

Morita: Ii **nekutai** desu ne. Atarashii-no desu-ka.

Sumisu: Jitsu-wa furui **nekutai** desu, yo. Sannen mae-ni **Hanabusa-san**-ga kureta-no desu.

Morita: Sō desu-ka. Sono tokei-mo sō desu-ka.

Sumisu: Iie, kono tokei-wa **Kitamura-san-no okā-san**-ni itadakimashita.

1. kabin, Hara-san, Hanabusa-san
2. sētā, Yagi-san, sensei
3. bōshi, Kitamura-san-no otō-san, sensei
4. hon, Mōri-san-no oku-san, Ishihara-san

SELF TEST

Translate the following sentences into Japanese:

1. My father gave me this clock.

2. I received a clock from my younger brother.

3. My teacher gave me a dictionary.

4. I recieved a pen from my teacher.

5. My mother lives in America (humble).

6. I have been in your way.

7. Please don't bother.

8. My younger sister is fourteen years old.

9. I think my older brother wants to come to Japan.

10. The teacher, Mr. Morita, went to my father's house.

LESSON NINETEEN
TSURETE ITTE KUREMASHITA

In this lesson you will learn:

- Giving verbs

- How to say a favor was given

- The plain -mashō verb form

- How to state that you would like another person to do something

DIALOGUE

A: あなたが かった にほんの おみやげは だれに あげるの ですか。

B: らいげつ わたしの ははの たんじょうび な ので、ははに あげよう と おもいます。

A: どこで かいましたか。

B: にほんの おみやげやで かいました。たなかさんが つれて いって くれました。

A: いつ おくるの ですか。

B: きょう ゆうびんきょくに もって いきたいの ですが、じかんが ないの です。

A: ああ、それ なら わたしが ゆうびんきょくの ちかくに いく ので かわりに もって いって あげましょう。

B: ごめいわく では ありませんか。

A: かまいませんよ。こうくうびんと ふなびんの どちらで おくりたい の ですか。

B: たんじょうび までに まにあわせたい ので、こうくうびんで おくりたい です。

A: はい わかりました。

B: ついでに この えはがきも だして もらえますか。

A: もちろん。きっては ありますか。

B: はい。ごしんせつ ありがとう ございます。

A: どう いたしまして。

A: *Anata-ga katta Nihon-no omiyage-wa dare-ni ageru-no desu-ka.*

A: To whom will you give the souvenir that you bought?

B: *Raigetsu watashi-no haha-no tanjōbi na node, haha-ni ageyō-to omoimasu.*

B: Next month is my mother's birthday, so I think I will give it to her.

A: *Doko-de kaimashita-ka.*

A: Where did you buy it?

B: *Nihon-no omiyageya-de kaimashita. Tanaka-san-ga tsurete itte kuremashita.*

B: At a Japanese souvenir shop. Mr. Tanaka did me the favor of taking me.

A: *Itsu okuru-no desu-ka.*

A: When will you send it?

B: *Kyō yūbinkyoku-ni motte ikitai-no desu ga, jikan-ga nai-no desu.*

B: I want to take it to the post office today, but I do not have enough time.

A: *Ā, sore nara, watashi-ga yūbinkyoku-no chikaku-ni iku node, kawari-ni motte itte agemashō.*

A: Well, I will be near the post office, so I can take it instead of you.

B: *Gomeiwaku dewa arimasen-ka.*

B: But wouldn't that be troublesome?

A: *Kamaimasen, yo. Kōkū-bin-to funabin-no dochira-de okuritai-no desu-ka.*

A: I do not mind. Do you want to send it by air or by sea?

B: *Tanjōbi made-ni maniawasetai node, kōkūbin-de okuritai desu.*

B: Well, I want it to reach her in time for her birthday, so I want to send it by air.

A: *Hai, wakarimashita.*

A: All right.

B: *Tsuide-ni kono ehagaki-mo dashite moraemasu-ka.*

B: While you are doing that, could you also mail this postcard for me?

A: *Mochiron. Kitte-wa arimasu-ka.*

A: Of course. Do you have a stamp?

B: *Hai. Go-shinsetsu arigatō gozaimasu.*

B: Yes. Thank you so much for doing me this favor.

A: *Dō itashimashite.*

A: It's no trouble.

When a plain verb is followed by *node*, it means "because . . ." ex. *Raishū chichi-no tanjōbi na* **node**, *okurimono-o kaimasu.* Because my father's birthday is next week, I will buy a gift.

175

atena
return address

dasu(-u)
to mail

e
picture

ehagaki
picture post card

funabin
sea mail

fūtō
envelope

gomeiwaku
troublesome

hagaki
postcard

harau(-u)
to pay

inu
dog

jūsho
address

kawari-ni
instead of

kitte
stamp

kōkū shokan
air letter

kōkūbin
airmail

kowaremono
fragile item

GRAMMAR EXPLANATION

1. Giving

For giving, three verbs may be used: *sashiagemasu, agemasu,* and *yarimasu.* The sentence pattern is:

> (Giver-**wa**) receiver-**ni** object-**o** **sashiagemasu.**
> **agemasu.**
> **yarimasu.**

sashiagemasu
to give to someone of a *higher* position:

  ex. Yagi-san-wa okurimono-o sensei-ni **sashiagemashita.**
  Mr. Yagi gave a present to the teacher.

agemasu
to give to someone of an *equal* position:

  ex. Watashi-wa hon-o tomodachi-ni **agemashita.**
  I gave a book to my friend.

yarimasu
to give to someone of a *lower* position, or someone from your family:

  ex. Watashi-wa imōto-ni kitte-o **yarimashita.**
  I gave a stamp to my sister.

2. Favors

When describing that someone did you a favor, or asking someone for a favor, use the -te verb form plus the giving and receiving verbs previously learned.

Kondo can be used to either mean "next time" or "this time." To determine which meaning is being used, pay attention to the context of the sentence.

Favor giver-*ga* receiver-*ni* object -*te* verb +
kudasaimasu.
or **kuremasu**.

Receiver-*wa* favor giver-*ni* object -*te* verb +
itadakimasu.
or **moraimasu**.

ex. *Sensei-ga (watashi-ni) tegami-o **kaite kudasaimashita**.*
The teacher did (gave) me the favor of writing a letter.

*Haha-ga (watashi-ni) jisho-o **katte kuremashita**.*
My mother did the favor of buying me a dictionary.

*(Watashi-wa) kyōju-ni Nihongo-o **oshiete itadakimashita**.*
I received a favor from my professor (which was) teaching me Japanese.

*(Watashi-wa) Hanabusa-san-ni kozutsumi-o **okutte moraimashita**.*
I received a favor from Mrs. Hanabusa (which was) sending the package.

177

kozutsumi
package, parcel

made-ni
in time

maniawaseru
to make it ready by

matsuri
festival

okuru(-u)
to send

omaneki
invitation

posuto
mail box, mail drop

saigo
the end

saisho
the beginning

sashiageru(-ru)
to give

shōsetsu
novel

sokutatsu
special delivery

tetsudau(-u)
to help

tsuide-ni
while you are at it

3. Plain -mashō

To change -mashō verbs into the plain form:

For -ru verbs: drop the final masu and add yō:

tabemasu	tabe**yō**
oshiemasu	oshie**yō**
shimasu	shi**yō**
agemasu	age**yō**

For -u verbs: drop the final u and add ō
Exception: Ending in tsu, drop tsu and add tō:

harau	hara**ō**
au	a**ō**
kau	ka**ō**
asobu	asob**ō**
iku	ik**ō**
yomu	yom**ō**
hashiru	hashir**ō**
sagasu	sagas**ō**
matsu	mat**ō**
tatsu	tat**ō**

Exception:	kuru	ko**yō**
	suru	**shiyō**

4. -Te hoshii

When you want another person to do something:

person-**ni** object -te verb **hoshii desu**.

ex. *Haha-ni kitte-o katte* **hoshii desu**.
I want my mother to buy a stamp.

Anata-ni watashi-to issho-ni pātī-ni itte
hoshii desu.
I want you to go to the party with me.

EXERCISES
1. Giving

Substitute the given words into the sentence:

Sashiagemasu

Watashi-wa **object**-*o* **receiver**-*ni sashiagemashita.*

Objects	Receiver
shōsetsu	Morita-san-no okā-san
fūtō	buchō
mōfu	Hara-san-no oku-san
jisho	sensei

Agemasu

Watashi-wa **object**-*o* **receiver**-*ni agemashita.*

Object	Receiver
tokei	Yagi-san
kagi	tomodachi
okane	Watanabe-san
hon	kyaku

Yarimasu

Watashi-wa **object**-*o* **receiver**-*ni yarimashita.*

Object	Receiver
gohan	inu
zubon	imōto
sētā	ane
iyahōn	otōto

Yaru
Yarimasu is not used frequently in Japanese, unless one is talking about giving something to an animal. If you are talking about a superior giving a gift to a subordinate, or giving within your family, *ageru* is all right to use.

179

tsurete iku
to take and show

yaru(-u)
to give

yorokonde iru
be happy to

COUNTRIES

Chūgoku
China

Furansu
France

Igirisu
England

Indo
India

Itaria
Italy

Kanada
Canada

Kankoku
Korea

Kita-Chōsen
North Korea

Oranda
Holland

2. Receiving favors

Choose the appropriate terms for each of the following sentences:

Imai-san-wa **giver**-*ni* **obj.+-te verb** *itadakimashita.*
Imai-san-wa **giver**-*ni* **obj.+-te verb** *moraimashita.*

Giver	Object, verb
imōto	*matsuri-ni tsurete iku*
Yamamoto sensei	*Nihongo-no hon-o kau*
Hara sensei-no oku-san	*shashin-o toru*
Yamada-san	*hagaki-o okuru*
watashi-no chichi	*shōsetsu-o kau*

Giver-*ga Hara-san-ni* **obj.+-te verb** *kudasaimashita.*
Giver-*ga Hara-san-ni* **obj.+-te verb** *kuremashita.*

Giver	Object, verb
buchō	*ringo-o kau*
Kitamura-san	*jisho-o hiku*
sensei	*oshieru*
Yōsuke-kun	*kūkō-e mukae-ni iku*
Kōsuke-kun	*katarogu-o watasu*

3. Plain -mashō

Conjugate the following verbs into the plain *mashō* form and substitute them into the sentences:

ex. jisho-o hiku

A: ***Jisho-o hikimashō**-ka.*

B: *Ē, **hikō**-to omoimasu.*

tsuku	*watasu*
asobu	*okuru*
sake-o nomu	*matsu*
benkyō suru	*omaneki-o suru*
itadaku	*uru*
miru	*kiku*
oeru	*isu-ni suwaru*
ageru	*shōsetsu-o kau*

When Japanese people point to themselves, they touch their noses, not their chests.

4. -Te hoshii

Change the sentences into the *-te hoshii* form:

ex. Kono hagaki-o yūbinkyoku-ni motte ikitai desu.

➡ *Anata-ni **kono hagaki-o yūbinkyoku-ni motte itte** hoshii desu.*

Tanjōbi-no pātī-ni ikitai desu.
Fūtō-ni jūsho-o kakitai desu.
Kaita kanji-o naoshitai desu.
Kono tegami-o okuritai desu.
Hara-san-o kūkō-ni mukae-ni ikitai desu.

SHORT DIALOGUES

1. *ex.* sensei, sashiageru

Tokuichiro:Nobushige-san, anata-wa mō
sensei*-ni shōsetsu-o*
sashiagemashita*-ka.*
Nobushige: Iie, **sensei***-ni shōsetsu-o*
sashiagemasen *deshita.*
Tokuichiro:Jā, ashita **sensei***-ni shōsetsu-o*
sashiageru *hō-ga ii-to*
omoimasu, yo.
Nobushige: Hai, sō shimashō.

1. tomodachi, ageru
2. Kankoku-no kata, ageru
3. Yamashita-san, sashiageru
4. buchō, sashiageru

2. *ex.* ehagaki, okuru, morau

Hiroko: *Anata-wa* **ehagaki***-o mō*
                okurimashita*-ka.*
Sachiko: *Jikan-ga nakatta node, Yamashita-*
                san-ni **okutte moraimashita**
Hiroko: *Sō desu-ka. Itsumo Yamashita-*
                san-ni iroirona koto-o shite
                moratte iru*-no desu, ne.*
Sachiko: *Ē, honto-ni sō desu. Yamashita-*
                san-wa shinsetsuna hito desu.

1. kozutsumi, kōkūbin-ni suru, itadaku
2. tegami, dasu, morau
3. kitte, kau, itadaku
4. kozutsumi, funabin-ni suru, morau

3. *ex.* tegami, kaku, sensei, kudasaru

> Hirakawa: **Tegami**-o mō **kakimashita**-ka.
> Sumisu: Hai, **kakimashita**.
> Hirakawa: Jibun-de **kakimashita**-ka.
> Sumisu: Saisho jibun-de **kakimashita** kedo, totemo muzukashikatta desu; soshite, saigo-ni **sensei**-ga tetsudatte **kudasaimashita**.
> Hirakawa: Itsumo **sensei**-ga tetsudatte **kudasaimasu**-ka.
> Sumisu: Iie. Jibun-de yaru hō-ga ii-no desu-ga, wakaranai toki-wa, **sensei**-ga tetsudatte **kudasaimasu**.

1. kanji-o yomu, Hirakawa sensei, kudasaru
2. shinbun-o yomu, Yamada-san, kureru
3. tegami-o kaku, tomodachi, kureru
4. hanashi-o suru, Hara-san, kudasaru

Don't be loud in public! Because their country is so crowded, Japanese people are extremely polite in public, which includes talking in low voices. When you are in public areas, speak quietly to those around you. Do NOT speak on your cell phone when using public transportation or in any area that is quiet.

At some train stations during rush hour, there are "pushers" who cram as many people as possible into the train cars. Because of this, some cars are now designated for females and children only. Take note of these signs when entering the train.

SELF-TEST

Translate the following sentences into Japanese:

1. The teacher helped me write the speech.

2. Mr. Matsumoto did the favor of taking me to the post office.

3. I gave a novel to my teacher, Mrs. Morimoto.

4. I gave a Japanese book to my younger sister.

5. I want Mr. Morita to mail this postcard.

Fill in the blanks with *wa, ni, o, ga, o, to,* or X:

6. Watashi ___ haha ___ bideo ___ agemashita.

7. Watashi ___ sensei ___ jisho ___ sashiagemashita.

8. Chichi ___ watashi ___ hon ___ katte ___ kuremashita.

9. Anata ___ kore ___ mite ___ hoshii desu.

10. Kyō ___ Mitsutake-san ___ koko ___ kuru ___ omoimasu.

LESSON TWENTY
TOMENAIDE KUDASAI

In this lesson you will learn:

- The -naide kudasai verb form

- How to ask for permission

- How to state yours or another's plans

DIALOGUE

I

スミス: とうきょう きょうと かんの おうふく きっぷを いちまい
ください。いきは あしたの とうきょう はつ よじ、そして
かえりは あさっての きょうと はつ にじは ありますか。

B: とうきょう はつ ごじ でも いい ですか。

スミス: ええ いい です。

B: はい。いちまん ごせん えん です。しんかんせんの
ホーム うむは じゅうごばん せん です。

スミス: はい わかりました。

つぎの ひ

いまい: きょうは どこに いくの ですか。

スミス: きょうとに いく つもり です。

いまい: なんじに でますか。

スミス: ごじ はつの しんかんせん です。

いまい: じかんは どの ぐらい かかりますか。

スミス: いちじかん はんで つく はず です。

II

スミス: うんてんしゅさん きょうと ホテル まで おねがい します。

うんてんしゅさん: はい。この こうさてんの てまえで も いい
ですか。ホテルは この みぎ がわに あります から。

スミス: そんな ところで とめないで ください。どこかで ユーターン
して ホテルの ちゅうしゃじょう まで いって ください。

うんてんしゅさん: はい わかりました。

I

Sumisu: *Tōkyō Kyōto kan-no ōfuku kippu-o ichimai kudasai. Iki-wa ashita-no Tōkyō hatsu yoji, soshite kaeri-wa asatte-no Kyōto hatsu niji-wa arimasu-ka.*

I

Smith: I would like to buy a round trip ticket from Tokyo to Kyoto please. Do you have one that leaves Tokyo tomorrow at 4:00 and returns from Kyoto the day after tomorrow at 2:00?

B: *Tōkyō hatsu goji demo ii desu-ka.*

S: *Ē, ii desu.*

B: *Hai. Ichiman gosen en desu. Shinkansen-no hōmu-wa jūgoban sen desu.*

S: *Hai, wakarimashita.*

Tsugi-no hi

Imai: *Kyō-wa doko-ni iku-no desu-ka.*

S: *Kyōto-ni iku tsumori desu.*

I: *Nanji-ni demasu-ka.*

S: *Goji hatsu-no shinkansen desu.*

I: *Jikan-wa dono gurai kakarimasu-ka.*

S: *Ichijikan han-de tsuku hazu desu.*

II

Sumisu: *Untenshu-san, Kyōto hoteru made onegai shimasu.*

Untenshu-san: *Hai. Kono kōsaten-no temae-de mo ii desu-ka. Hoteru-wa kono migi gawa-ni arimasu kara.*

S: *Sonna tokoro-de tomenaide kudasai.*

B: Would 5:00 from Tokyo be all right?

S: Yes, that's fine.

B: All right. It is 15,000 yen. The bullet train's platform line is number 15.

S: O.K.

The next day

Imai: Where are you going today?

S: I'm planning to go to Kyoto.

I: What time do you leave?

S: On the 5:00 bullet train.

I: How long will it take?

S: It's expected to take one and a half hours.

II

Smith: Driver, please take me to the Kyoto Hotel.

Driver: Of course. May I stop just before this intersection? The hotel is on the right side of the street.

S: Please do not stop there. Please do a

Addresses
Addresses are made up of the city, *shi*, place name, *machi* or *chō*, then *chōme* (divisions of *machi* or *chō*) + *banchi* (sections of *chōme*) + *gō* (house number). *ex. Tachikawa-shi, Ogawa-chō, san-chōme, go-banchi, hyakunana-gō.*

187

arubaito
part-time job

chūsha kinshi
no parking

chūshajō
parking lot

deguchi
exit

hatsu
departure time

hazu
it's expected

hidari
left

hidari gawa
left side

hōmu
platform

kado
corner

kochiragawa
this side

kōsaten
intersection

kotoshi
this year

kure
the end of the year

Dokoka-de yū tān shite hoteru-no chūshajō made itte kudasai.

U: *Hai, wakarimashita.*

u-turn somewhere and go to the parking lot of the hotel.

D: Yes, I understand.

GRAMMAR EXPLANATION

1. -Naide kudasai

The negative form of *kudasai* is *-naide kudasai*. It is formed by using the *nai* form of plain verbs and adding *-de kudasai*.

> *ex. takushī-o tomenai*
> the taxi does not stop
> *takushī-o tomenaide kudasai*
> please do not stop the taxi
>
> *sashiagenai*
> does not give
> *sashiagenaide kudasai*
> please do not give

2. -Te mo ii desu-ka

To ask someone if it is alright to do something, use:

-te verb + *mo ii desu-ka.*

> *ex. Itte mo ii desu-ka.*
> Is it all right to go?
>
> *Tabete mo ii desu-ka.*
> Is it all right to eat?

Common ways to answer are:
1. The -*te* verb form + *mo ii desu.*
    Itte mo ii desu.
    It is all right to go.

    Tabete mo ii desu.
    It is all right to eat.

2. *Hai, kamaimasen.*
    Yes, I do not mind.

3. The -*naide kudasai* phrase.
    ikanaide kudasai
    Please do not go.

    tabenaide kudasai
    Please do not eat.

4. A -*te* verb + -*wa ikemasen* means an action is prohibited or impossible.
    itte-wa ikemasen
    not allowed to go

    tabete-wa ikemasen
    not allowed to eat

Verbs can be used as subjects if the -*masu* ending is dropped.

From the Airport
When visiting Japan, one of the cheapest and fastest ways to travel from Narita airport to Tokyo is by train. The bus is also quite clean and inexpensive, but can get stuck in traffic. No matter your mode of transport, while in route do not use your cell phone or speak loudly to those around you.

magaru(-u)
to turn

-mai
counter for
papers,
tickets, plates

massugu
straight ahead

migi
right
(direction)

mukōgawa
across the
street

noriba
boarding
place

ōfuku
round trip

otsuri
change
(money)

ryōri
cuisine

shingō
traffic light

shokudō
cafeteria

temae
just before

tomaru(-u)
to stop at (no
object)

tomeru(-ru)
to stop, park
(needs object)

3. Tsumori, yotei, hazu

When **you** plan to do something, use:

> plain verb + *tsumori desu*

*ex. Ashita watashi-wa Igirisu-ni kono
kozutsumi-o okuru **tsumori desu.***
Tomorrow, I plan to send this package to
England.

*Kyō watashi-wa koko-o rokuji-ni deru
tsumori desu.*
Today I plan to leave here at 6:00.

To state **yours** or **another's** plans:

> plain verb + *yotei desu*

*ex. Raigetsu-no kokonoka-wa Sumisu-san-no
imōto-san-no tanjōbi desu kara, hon-o
kau **yotei desu.***
Because Ms. Smith's sister's birthday is
next month on the ninth, (I) plan to buy
(her) a book.

*Tanaka-san-wa Chūgoku-de
Chūgokugo-o benkyō suru **yotei desu.***
Mr. Tanaka plans to study Chinese in China.

To say that something is expected:

> plain verb + *hazu desu*

*ex. Hikōki-wa sanji gojuppun-ni koko-ni
tsuku **hazu desu.***

The plane is expected to arrive here at 3:50.

*Eiga-wa goji-ni hajimaru **hazu desu**.*
The movie is expected to begin at 5:00.

4. -Te . . .

Another way to connect sentences is to use the *-te* form for the verb in the first sentence, then state the second sentence.

> *ex. Anata-no namae-o **kaite** suwatte kudasai.*
> Please write your name and sit down.

> *Watashi-wa kitte-o **katte** hagaki-o okurimashita.*
> I bought a stamp and mailed the postcard.

Yotei
To ask someone if they have any plans, use *nanika yotei-ga arimasu-ka.* "Do you have any particular plans?"

EXERCISES
1. -Te mo ii desu-ka, -naide kudasai

Place the following phrases into the given sentences:

> *ex. densha-no naka-de o-bentō-o taberu*
> A: **Densha-no naka-de o-bentō-o tabete** *mo ii desu-ka.*
> B: *Ā,* **tabenaide** *kudasai.*
>
> *koko-de tabako-o sū*
> *kono ehagaki-o okuru*
> *kono taoru-o tsukau*
> *ano kado-de tomaru*
> *ano kōsaten-de hidari-ni magaru*

tsuku(-u)
to arrive

tsumori
plan

umi
sea

untenshu-san
driver

yama
mountain

yukkuri
slowly,
leisurely

**MODES OF
TRANSPORT:**
basu
bus

chikatetsu
subway

michi
road, street

shinkansen
bullet train

takushī
taxi

tetsudō
railway

2. -Te mo ii desu

Place the following phrases into the given
sentences:

> *ex. basu-de yama-ni iku*
> A: **Basu-de yama-ni itte** *mo ii desu-ka.*
> B: *Ē,* **itte** *mo ii desu.*

> *umi-de oyogu*
> *buchō-san, kyō hachiji-ni uchi-ni kaeru*
> *kono hagaki-o Kanada-ni okuru*
> *Tanaka-san-no nōto-ni kaku*
> *sono deguchi kara deru*
> *o-kyaku-san, asoko-no chūshajō-de
> tomaru*

3. Tsumori, yotei, hazu

Change the sentences into the *hazu desu* form:

> *ex. Basu-wa kuji-ni kimasu.*
> ➡ *Basu-wa kuji-ni kuru hazu desu.*

> *Sumisu-san-wa kokonoka-ni Ōsaka-ni
> ikimasu.*
> *Purojekuto-wa raishū-no getsuyōbi-
> ni owarimasu.*
> *Asatte haha-ga tazunete kimasu.*
> *Hiruton hoteru-de pātī-o shimasu.*

Place the following phrases into both sentences:

> *ex. Nihon-ni ikimasu*
> ➡ *Watashi-wa **Nihon-ni iku** tsumori desu.*
> ➡ *Tanaka-san-wa **Nihon-ni iku** yotei desu.*

> Sumisu-san-ga yūbe mita eiga-o
> mimasu.
> Hara-san-ga hoshigatte ita bideo-o
> kaimasu.
> Sensei-no kaita hon-o yomimasu.
> Rekishi-o benkyō shimasu.
> Chikatetsu-de Tōkyō-ni ikimasu.

-de
Use *de* as the particle when explaining how you went or came. *ex. Basu-de* kimashita, came by bus. *Takushī-de uchi-ni kaerimashita*, came home by taxi.

4. -Te . . .

Combine the given sentences into one sentence using the -te . . . form:

> *ex. E-o kaimasu. Uchi-ni kaerimasu.*
> ➡ *E-o katte uchi-ni kaerimasu.*

> Mise-ni ikimasu. Yamada-san-ni
> aimasu.
> Omiyageya-ni ikimasu. Omiyage-o
> kaimasu.
> Gorufu-o shimasu. Tenisu-o shimasu.
> Taoru-o kaimasu. Tomodachi-ni sono
> taoru-o agemasu.
> Hara-san-no ie-ni ikimasu. Hara-san-
> to iroirona koto-o hanashimasu.

Taxi doors in Japan close by themselves. They are controlled by the driver.

SHORT DIALOGUES

1. *ex.* densha, oishii resutoran, resutoran-ni iku

A: *Nagai aida machimashita-ka.*
B: *Iie, sakki tsukimashita.*
A: *Basu-de kimashita-ka.*
B: *Iie, **densha**-de kimashita.*
A: *Mukōgawa-ni **oishii resutoran**-ga arimasu ne. Sono **resutoran-ni itte** mo ii desu-ka.*
B: *Hai, sono **resutoran**-ga ii desu.*

1. takushī, ii eigakan, eiga-o miru
2. kuruma, subarashii resutoran, resutoran-de taberu
3. densha, sugoi kissaten, kissaten-ni iku
4. takushī, ii depāto, depāto-ni iku

2. *ex.* kanji-o benkyō suru, Nihongo-no gakkō-ni iku

I: *Sumisu-san-wa itsu made Nihon-ni imasu-ka.*
S: *Kotoshi-no kure made iru tsumori desu.*
I: *Sono-aida-ni nanika yotei-ga arimasu-ka.*
S: ***Kanji-o benkyō suru** yotei desu.*
I: *Ii desu ne. Hajimete Nihon-ni kita toki **Nihongo-no gakkō-ni iku**-no-wa taihen deshita-ka.*
S: *Sukoshi taihen deshita, sorede tomodachi-ga tetsudatte kuremashita.*

1. Nihongo-o benkyō suru, apāto-o kariru
2. Eigo-o oshieru, densha-ni noru
3. Iroirona yūmeina tokoro-o tazuneru,
   Nihongo-o hanasu
4. Mitsubishi ginkō-ni tsutomeru,
   arubaito-o sagasu
5. Tanaka-san-no ie-ni sumu, Nihongo-o
   hanasu

3. *ex.* kado, magaru, kissaten-no mae-de, tomaru

Jonson: *Doko-de takushī-ni noremasu-ka.*
Hara: *Asoko-no takushī noriba-de*
takushī-ni noremasu yo.
Jonson: *Arigatō gozaimasu.*
Kono jūsho made tsurete itte
kudasai.
Untenshu-san: Hai, wakarimashita.
Jonson: *Motto yukkuri unten shite kudasai.*
Untenshu-san: Hai. O-kyaku-san, ano **kado**-
de **magatte** *mo ii desu-ka.*
Jonson: *Ā.* **Magaranaide** *kudasai. Ano*
kissaten-no mae-de **tomaru** *hō-*
ga ii desu yo.
Untenshu-san: Hai, wakarimashita.
1. shingō, tomaru, kōsaten-de hidari-ni
   magaru
2. kado, tomaru, chūshajō-de tomaru
3. kado, magaru, shokudō-no mae-de tomaru
4. kōsaten, magaru, mise-no mae-de
   tomaru

SELF-TEST

Translate the following sentences into Japanese:

1. Please do not turn at that corner.

2. The bus is expected to stop here at 3:00.

3. Is it alright if I eat the food you made?

4. The day after tomorrow, I plan to go skiing, and play tennis (use -te...).

5. You cannot turn right at this corner.

Unscramble the following sentences:

6. kono ka no temae de ii yū tān kōsaten desu shite mo.

7. desu Kyōto mo ni itte de densha ii ka.

8. oeru desu wa kyō ni o watashi tsumori hachiji shigoto.

9. kudasai san kochiraga wa untenshu tomaranaide de.

10. ni itte Tōkyō o kaimasu tokei.

LESSON TWENTY ONE
HIRAKANAKUTE-WA IKEMASEN

In this lesson you will learn:

- The -tari/dari expression
- The -nakute-wa ikemasen verb form
- The -te mimasu verb phrase

DIALOGUE

I

ジョンソン: いま いそがしい ですか。

いまい: いいえ、ただ ほんを よんだり テレビを みたり して いる だけ です。なにか てつだいましょうか。

ジョンソン: ええ。じつは ぎんこうへ いって ドルを えんに りょうがえ しなければ なりません。それ から こうざを ひらかなくては いけません。てつだって くださいますか。

いまい: もちろん。いま から いきましょうか。

ジョンソン: そう して くれますか。にほんでは ふつう よきん にも りしが つきますか。

いまい: すこし。でも たしか では ありません。いって みましょう。

II

ジョンソン: この ドルを えんに りょうがえ したいの ですが。

B: わかりました。かわせ レートは いち ドル ひゃく じゅう えん で てすうりょうが ご パーセント です。はい、どうぞ。

ジョンソン: ありがとう ございます。

ジョンソン: あのう こうざを ひらきたいの ですが。

B: わかりました。この かみに きにゅう して ください。これが あなたの よきん つうちょう です。あなたの キャッシュ カード を あとで おくります。げんきんを ひきだしたり にゅうきん したり する とき その カードを つかって ください。

ジョンソン: はい わかりました。

B: いっかげつに いちど あなたの ざんだかを きにゅう した けいさんしょを おくります。それで おかねの だしいれと おりしの めいさいが わかります。

I	**I**
Jonson: *Ima isogashii desu-ka.*	Johnson: Are you busy now?
Imai: *Iie, tada hon-o yondari terebi-o mitari shite iru dake desu. Nanika tetsudaimashō-ka.*	Imai: No, I'm just reading a book and watching TV. Do you want me to help you with something?

J: *Ē, jitsu-wa ginkō-e itte doru-o en-ni ryōgae shinakereba narimasen. Sore kara kōza-o hiraka-nakute-wa ikemasen. Tetsudatte kudasaimasu-ka.*

J: Yes, actually I need to go to a bank and change my dollars into yen, and then I need to open an account. Could you help me?

I: *Mochiron. Ima kara ikimashō-ka.*

I: Of course. Shall we go now?

J: *Sō shite kuremasu-ka. Nihon-dewa futsū yokin ni-mo rishi-ga tsukimasu-ka.*

J: You will do me this favor? In Japan, do banks also pay you interest when you have an account?

I: *Sukoshi, demo tashika dewa arimasen. Itte mimashō.*

I: A little, but I'm not certain. Let's go and see.

II

II

J: *Kono doru-o en-ni ryōgae shitai-no desu ga.*

J: I would like to change these dollars into yen.

B: *Wakarimashita. Kawase rēto-wa ichi doru hyaku jū en de tesūryo-ga go pāsento desu. Hai, dōzo.*

B: I understand. The exchange rate is one hundred ten yen for one dollar, plus there is a five percent charge. Here you are.

J: *Arigatō gozaimasu.*

J: Thank you.

J: *Anō, kōza-o hirakitai-no desu ga.*

J: I would like to open an account.

B: *Wakarimashita. Kono kami-ni ki'nyū shite kudasai. Kore-ga anata-no yokin tsūchō desu. Anata-no kyasshu kādo-o ato de okurimasu. Genkin-o*

B: All right, please fill out these papers. This is your bank book. Your money card will be sent to you later. When you need to withdraw cash or make

ano(o)
well . . .

arau(-u)
to wash

betsu betsu ni
separately

dashiire
deposit and withdraw

de
is...and

denki
light, electricity

doru
dollar

futsū yokin
savings account

(go) yō
something one needs to do

hikidasu(-u)
to withdraw

hiraku(-u)
to open

ka
or

kādo
card

hikidashitari nyū-
kin shitari suru toki
sono kādo-o tsukatte
kudasai.

J: Hai, wakarimashita.

B: Ikkagetsu-ni ichi-do
anata-no zandaka-o
ki'nyū shita keisansho-o
okurimasu. Sorede
okane-no dashiire-to
o-rishi-no meisai-ga
wakarimasu.

a deposit, please use
that card.

J: All right.

B: Once a month (we) will
send you a statement
that will show your
balance. Also, it
will show all your
transactions and the
details of your interest.

GRAMMAR EXPLANATION

1. Tari/dari

When a verb+*tari/dari* and another verb+*tari/dari*
+*shite imasu* are used in a sentence, it means
that one has been doing these things back and
forth for a while. To form this pattern, add *ri* to the
plain past verb.

ex. *Kyō-wa keiki-o tsukuttari hon-o yondari
shite imasu.*
Today I've been making a cake, reading a
book, making a cake, and reading a book.

*Sono kaisha-wa iroirona seihin-o yunyū
shitari yushutsu shitari shite imasu.*
That company imports and exports
various products.

2. Nakute, nakereba

There are two different expressions to state that

200

one has to do something. They differ from the *nasai* verb form studied previously in that *nasai* is a command given, whereas this verb form is not necessarily ordered.

Nakute-wa ikemasen

To form this pattern, use the plain negative form of verbs, and instead of using *nai* as the ending, use *nakute-wa ikemasen*.

> ex. *ikanai*
>
>   *ginkō-ni ika**nakute-wa ikemasen***
>   have to go to the bank
>
>   *orosanai*
>   *genkin-o orosa**nakute-wa ikemasen***
>   have to withdraw cash
>
>   *tsukawanai*
>   *kurejitto kādo-o tsukawa**nakute-wa ikemasen***
>   have to use a credit card

Nakereba narimasen

The meaning and grammar structure for this expression are exactly the same as for *nakute-wa ikemasen*. Use *nakereba narimasen* after dropping *nai*.

> ex. *hanasanai*
>   *sensei-to hanasa**nakereba narimasen***
>   have to talk with the teacher

When using *nakereba narimasen* or *nakute-wa ikemasen*, you are stating that you have to do something. Literally, it means that if you do not do it, you will be in a bad situation.

kawase rēto
exchange rate

keisansho
statement

kesu(-u)
to turn off

kimatte iru
it has been
decided

ki'nyū suru
to fill out

kō yū
that kind of

kōza
account

**kurejitto
kādo**
credit card

**kyasshu
kādo**
money card

meisai
details

modoru(-u)
to return

nyūkin
deposit

orosu(-u)
to withdraw

pāsento
percent

pēji
page

harawanai
zeikin-o harawanakereba narimasen
have to pay taxes

shinai
en-o doru-ni ryōgae shinakereba
narimasen
have to change yen into dollars

3. -Te mimasu

When the -*te* verb is used with *mimasu*, the meaning becomes "try _____ and see."

> ex. *Juppēji made yonde mimasu.*
> I will read to page 10 and see (if I like it).

When used with *mimashō*, the nuance changes to "let's try _____ and see."

> ex. *Sono resutoran-de tabete mimashō.*
> Let's try eating at that restaurant and see (if we like it, if it's good, etc.).

EXERCISES
1. Tari/dari

Combine the following verbs and place them into the given sentence:

> ex. *Supeingo-o benkyō suru, rajio-o kiku*
> ➡ *Boku-wa* **Supeingo-o benkyō shitari rajio-o kiitari** *shite imasu.*
>
> *shinbun-o yomu, rajio-o kiku*
> *o-kashi-o taberu, mizu-o nomu*

tegami-o kaku, jisho-o hiku

takushī-ni noru, basu-ni noru

gohan-o tsukuru, sōji-o suru

2. Nakute-wa ikemasen, nakereba naranai

Change the following phrases into the *nakute-wa ikemasen* and *nakereba narimasen* forms:

ex. sōji-o suru

➡ *sōji-o shinakute-wa ikemasen*

➡ *sōji-o shinakereba narimasen*

denki-o kesu

kozutsumi-o okuru

megane-o kakeru

doa-o shimeru

kuruma-o arau

isoide imasu kara sugu-ni dekakeru

toshokan-ni hon-o kaesu

ane-o kūkō-e mukae-ni iku

To convert one currency into another, use: Currency 1-*o* currency 2-*ni* *ryōgae shite kudasai. ex. En-***o*** *doru*-***ni*** ***ryōgae shite kudasai***. Please change the yen to dollars.

3. Matching

Match the following phrases:

1. *Akaruku narimashita kara denki-o* A. *shimenakereba narimasen*
2. *Samuku narimashita kara doa-o* B. *tsukenakute-wa ikemasen*
3. *Asatte tesuto-ga arimasu kara* C. *kesanakereba narimasen*
4. *Nodo-ga kawakimashita kara mizu-o* D. *nomanakute-wa ikemasen*
5. *Samuku narimashita kara sutōbu-o* E. *benkyō shinakereba narimasen*
6. *Takusan tabemashita kara* F. *jogingu-o shinakute-wa ikemasen.*

rishi
interest

-ryo, ryōkin
charge, fee

ryōgae suru
to exchange,
change
money

shimeru(-ru)
to close

sōji suru
to clean

sutōbu
wood-burning
stove, furnace

tada
just

teiki yokin
fixed time
deposit

tesūryo
service fee

tōza yokin
checking
account

tsuku(-u)
to pay

tsumetai(i)
cool (when
touched)

4. -Te mimasu

Change the following sentences into the *-te*
mimashō form:

ex. kanji-o kaku
➡ *kanji-o kaite mimashō*

Michiko-san-ga suki datta ongakukai-ni iku
Nihon ryōri-o tsukuru
Hara-san-no tsukutta ryōri-o taberu
Mitsubishi-no kuruma-no katarogu-o yomu

SHORT DIALOGUES

1. *ex.* bun-o kaku

A: *Ima o-isogashii desu-ka.*
B: *Sukoshi isogashii desu. Kyō-wa o-kyaku-
san-ga kuru node, sōji-o shitari gohan-o
tsukuttari shite imasu, yo. Nanika go-yō
desu-ka.*
A: *Anō, jitsu-wa Nihongo-de **bun-o kaite**
imasu node, chotto naoshite
kudasaimasu-ka.*
B: *Ii desu yo. Kono **bun**-wa jōzu desu, yo.
Nagai aida **kaite** ita-no desu-ka.*
A: *Hai. Kyō ichinichijū **bun-o kaitari**
jisho-o hitari shite imashita. Arigatō
gozaimashita.*
B: *Dō itashimashite.*

1. kanji-o kaku
2. shukudai-o suru
3. tegami-o kaku

2. *ex.* yūgata haha-ga kuru, kūkō-e mukae-ni iku,
denki-o kesu

   A: *Ima kara o-hima desu-ka.*
   B: *Iie. **Yūgata haha-ga kimasu** node,
      Kūkō-e mukai-ni ikanakereba
      narimasen.*
   A: *Sō desu-ka. Watashi-mo issho-ni
      ikimashō-ka.*
   B: *Demo gomeiwaku deshō . . .*
   A: *Ii desu yo. Ima iku hō-ga ii desu-ka.*
   B: *Chotto matte kudasai. **Denki-o
      kesanakute**-wa ikemasen kara.*

    1. senshū hon-o karita, Yagi-san-no ie-ni
       iku, doa-o shimeru
    2. ototoi katta saifu-o kaesu, mise-ni iku,
       terebi-o kesu
    3. raigetsu chichi-no tanjōbi desu,
       okurimono-o kau, denki-o kesu
    4. konban haha-ga kuru, eki-e mukae-ni
       iku, mado-o shimeru

tsutsumu(-u)
to wrap

yokin
savings,
deposit

yokin tsūchō
bank book

zandaka
balance

zeikin
tax

3. *ex.* ongakukai-no kippu, iku, ongakukai-ni iku

A: ***Ongakukai-no kippu**-ga aru-no desu ga.*
*Issho-ni **ikimasen**-ka.*
B: *Sō desu ne. Kō yū **ongakukai-ni itta**
koto-ga arimasen.*
A: *Watashi-mo sō desu yo. **Itte** mimashō-ka.*
B: *Sō shimashō.*
A: *Anata-ni okane-o harawanakereba narimasen.*
B: *Kekkō desu. Harawanakute-mo ii desu.*
A: *Hontō desu-ka.*
B: *Mochiron.*

1. kowai eiga-no kippu, miru, eiga-o miru
2. Furansu-no keiki, taberu, keiki-o taberu
3. geki-no kippu, iku, geki-ni iku
4. rokku konsāto-no kippu, iku, konsāto-ni iku

SELF-TEST
Translate the following sentences into Japanese:

1. Today, I've been reading the newspaper and making sushi.

2. To withdraw cash, I have to use this cash card.

3. I have to buy a gift for my mother.

4. I have to read to page 40.

5. Please change the yen into dollars.

6. Let's try going to the restaurant Mr. Morita liked.

7. Let's try eating the food my husband made.

8. The baby eats and sleeps, eats and sleeps.

9. It has become hot, so I must open the window.

10. I have to open an account.

LESSON TWENTY TWO
SUWARASETE ITADAKIMASU

In this lesson you will learn:

- The -seru, -saseru verb form
- The -sō desu phrase
- The -sōna adjective expression

DIALOGUE

I

ジョンソン: こんにちは。わたしは アイビーエムの ジョンソン です。
はなぶささんと にじに おやくそく して いるの ですが。

さくらい: いらっしゃいませ。はなぶさは ただいま かいぎ
ちゅうで ございます。

ジョンソン: つごうが わるいの でしょうか。

さくらい: いいえ。にじ すぎには おわると もうして おりました。
どうぞおかけに なって ください。

ジョンソン: はい すわらせて いただきます。

さくらい: コーヒーは いかが ですか。

ジョンソン: ありがとう ございます。

さくらい: カタログを どうぞ。

ジョンソン: ありがとう ございます。おもしろそうな カタログ
ですね。あなたの かいしゃは さいきん
きゅうせいちょう して いる そう ですね。

さくらい: おかげさまで。

II

A: しごとの あとで みんなで しょくじに でかけようか。

B: いい ですね。

A: レストランで きょう みた スライドの しつもんに こたえよう。
それに ボーナスに ついても はなそう。

B: かちょうの いった こと きいたかい。

C: いや きかなかった。

B: しごとの あとで しょくじに でかけよう と いったよ。きみも
いくかい。

C: もちろん。

I

Jonson: *Konnichi-wa.
Watashi-wa Ai-Bī-Emu-no
Jonson desu. Hanabusa-
san-to niji-ni oyakusoku
shite iru-no desu ga.*

I

Johnson: Hello, I am Mr.
Johnson from IBM. I have
a 2:00 appointment with
Mr. Hanabusa.

Sakurai: *Irasshaimase.*
Hanabusa-san-wa
tadaima kaigi chū de
gozaimasu.

Sakurai: Welcome. (Mr.)
Hanabusa is in a
conference right now.

J: *Tsugō-ga warui-no*
deshō-ka.

J: Then it is a bad time?

S: *Iie. Niji sugi-ni-wa*
owaru-to mōshite
orimashita. Dōzo
o-kake-ni natte kudasai.

S: No, he said he would
be finished soon after
2:00. Please take a
seat.

J: *Hai, suwarasete*
itadakimasu.

J: With your permission, I
will.

S: *Kōhī-wa ikaga desu-*
ka.

S: Would you care for
coffee?

J: *Arigatō gozaimasu.*

J: Yes, thank you.

S: *Katarogu-o dōzo.*

S: Please have our catalogue.

J: *Arigatō gozaimasu.*
Omoshirosōna
katarogu desu, ne.
Anata-no kaisha-wa
saikin kyū-sei-chō
shite iru sō desu ne.

J: Thank you. This
is an interesting
looking catalogue. I
understand recently
your company has
been growing rapidly.

S: *Okagesamade.*

S: Thank goodness.

II

II

A: *Shigoto-no ato de*
minna-de shokuji-ni
dekakeyō-ka.

A: After work, would all
of you like to go out to
eat?

B: *Ii desu ne.*

B: Yes.

A: *Resutoran-de kyō mita*
suraido-no shitsumon-
ni kotaeyō. Sore-ni
bōnasu-ni tsuite-mo

A: While we are at the
restaurant, I will answer
your questions about
the slides we saw

**Company
Name**
To state which
company you
are from, say
Watashi-wa
company's
name-*no*, your
name *desu*.
ex. *Watashi-wa
Mitsubishi-no
Jonson desu.*
I am Miss
Johnson from
Mitsubishi.

Ai-Bī-Emu
IBM

atsumeru(-ru)
to gather

bikkuri suru
to be
surprised

bōnasu
bonus

gorufu
golf

hazukashii(i)
embarrased,
shy

honsha
headquarters

itteta
said

jōbu(na)
strong

kaigi chū de
in a
conference

kaigi shitsu
conference
room

kaigi suru
to have a
conference

katazukeru(-ru)
to finish up,
clean up

kawaii(i)
cute

kēsu
showcase

hanasō.

B: *Kachō-no itta koto
kiitakai.*

C: *Iya, kikanakatta.*

B: *Shigoto-no ato de
shokuji-ni dekakeyō-to
itteta yo. Kimi-mo ikukai.*

C: *Mochiron.*

today. We will also talk
about your bonuses.

B: Did you hear what the
section chief said?

C: No, I did not.

B: He said that after work
we will go out to eat.
Will you come with us?

C: Of course.

GRAMMAR EXPLANATION

1. -Seru, -saseru

When this verb form is used, it means that
someone makes or forces another to do
something. To form this pattern use plain negative
verbs:

For -*ru* verbs, drop the final *nai* and add *saseru*

    ex. *tabenai*

        *tabe**saseru***   makes one eat

        irenai

        *ire**saseru***   makes one pour

        konai

        *ko**saseru***   makes one come

For -*u* verbs, drop the final *nai* and add *seru*

    ex. *asobanai*

        *asoba**seru***   makes one play

        kakanai

        *kaka**seru***   makes one write

yomanai

yomaseru   makes one read

hanasanai

hanasaseru   makes one speak

awanai

awaseru   makes one meet

Exceptions: *shinai*   *saseru*

              minai   *miseru*

Grammar pattern for *-seru, -saseru* verbs:

> Subject-*wa* indirect object-*ni* object-*o -seru, -saseru* verb

ex. *Gakusei-wa Eigo-o benkyō shimasu.*
The student studies English.
Sensei-wa gakusei-ni Eigo-o benkyō **sasemasu**.
The teacher makes the student study English.

-Seru, -saseru itadakimasu

When you use the *seru, saseru* verb form
with *itadakimasu*, you are saying, "With your
permission, I will ____." In Japanese, it literally
means "given the favor of being allowed to____."

ex. *ika**sete itadakimasu***
with your permission, (I) will go

*mata**sete itadakimasu***
with your permission, (I) will wait

The *-seru, saseru* form of verbs usually implies that the person who makes another do something is a superior, like a boss making an employee do something, a teacher making a student do something, etc. It also can mean an older person makes a younger person do something, or that someone has been tricked or bribed into doing something.

keisan suru
to calculate

kikai
machine

kōfuku(na)
happy

kōsu
course

kotaeru(-ru)
to answer

kotoshi
this year

kyū
suddenly,
rapidly

Midori-ga oka
a golf course

mōsu(-u)
to say (humble)

nemui(i)
sleepy

Nippon
Japan (formal)

Nyū Yōku
New York

okagesa-made
thank
heavens,
thank all that
is good

o-kake-ni natte kudasai
please take a
seat (polite)

-Seru, -saseru kudasai

When this verb form is used with kudasai, it means, "Please allow me the favor of _____."

ex. **ikasete kudasai**
please allow (me) to go

matasete kudasai
please allow (me) to wait

2. Sō desu

When *sō desu* is used at the end of a sentence, it means that the speaker heard the information from somewhere, or understands that to be the case.

The following patterns can be used:

1. plain verb + *sō desu*
ex. *Sumisu-san-wa pātī-no toki bikkuri shita* **sō desu.**
I heard Ms. Smith was surprised during the party.

Tanaka-san-wa kitte-o atsumete iru **sō desu.**
I understand that Mr. Tanaka is collecting stamps.

2. *i* adjective + *sō desu*
ex. *Sono eiga-wa omoshiroi* **sō desu.**
I heard that movie is interesting.

Mitsutake-san-no kodomo-wa kawaii **sō desu.**
I heard that Mrs. Mitsutake's child is cute.

3. *na* adjective + *da* or *datta* + *sō desu*
   ex. *Matsumoto-san-wa genki datta **sō desu**.*
   I heard Mrs. Matsumoto is healthy.

   *Tanaka-san-to kekkon shita onnanohito-wa totemo kirei da **sō desu**.*
   I heard the woman Mr. Tanaka married is very beautiful.

-*sō* can also be combined with adjectives to state that something looks ____. For *i* adjectives, drop the final *i* before *sō desu*. When using *na* adjectives, drop the *na*.

ex. *oishi**sō***	looks delicious
*jōbu**sō***	looks strong
*nemu**sō***	looks sleepy
*jōzu**sō***	looks skillful
*kōfuku**sō***	looks happy
Exception: *yoi/ii*	*yosa**sō***

3. Adjective + sōna

To use the adjective + *sō* form to directly modify a noun, and add *na* to both *i* and *na* adjectives.

ex. *oishisō*	looks delicious
*oishisō**na** sakana*	delicious-looking fish
nemusō	looks tired
*nemusō**na** okā-san*	tired-looking mother
genkisō	looks healthy
*genkisō**na** kodomo*	healthy-looking child
kōfukusō	looks happy
*kōfukusō**na** hito*	happy-looking person

Be careful not to confuse *sō* adjectives with adjectives + *sō desu*. For example, *isogashisō* means "looks busy," while *isogashii sō desu* means "I understand that (someone) is busy."

213

sabishii(i)
lonely

seichō suru
to grow

semai(i)
narrow, small

shigoto-no
ato de
after work

shinjiru
(-ru)
to believe

sugi
(soon) after

suraido
slide

tadaima
just now

(o)tetsudai-
san
maid

tsugō
convenience

tsuite
concerning

tsumaranai(i)
boring

(o)yakusoku
suru
to make an
appointment
or reservation

yasai
vegetables

EXERCISES

1. -Seru, -saseru

Change the following sentences into the -seru, -saseru form:

ex. O-tetsudai-san-wa gohan-o tsukurimasu.
➡ O-tetsudai-san-ni gohan-o tsukurasemasu.

Gakusei-wa Nihongo-o hanashimasu.
Onnanoko-wa kusuri-o nomimasu.
Gakusei-wa Eigo-no hon-o yomimasu.
Otokonoko-wa eki-de machimasu.
Kodomotachi-wa yasai-o tabemasu.
Hirashain-wa purojekuto-o katazukemasu.

2. -Sete, -sasete itadakimasu

Change the following sentences into the -sete, -sasete itadakimasu form:

ex. Hara-san-no tsukutta gohan-o taberu.
➡ Hara-san-no tsukutta gohan-o tabesasete itadakimasu.

Hara-san-ga ireta ocha-o nomu
Isu-ni suwaru
Kaichō-no kaita tegami-o yomu
Kaigi-shitsu-de hanashi-o suru
Kono kikai-no setsumei-o suru
Jisho-o tsukau

3. -Sete, -sasete kudasai

Conjugate the given words into the -sete, -sasete

214

form and fill in the blank spaces:

matsu, tsukau, unten suru, kaeru, tetsudau

1. *Michiko-san-wa sugu-ni kuru deshō kara,*
   koko-de watashi-ni _____ kudasai.
2. *Kono purojekuto-wa muzukashii desu kara,*
   watashi-ni _____ kudasai.
3. *Watashi-no kuruma-ga aru node, _____ kudasai.*
4. *Anata-no denwa-o _____ kudasai.*
5. *Jūgofun hayaku shigoto-kara _____ kudasai.*

4. Sō desu

Match the following phrases:

1. *Asatte Yamada-san-wa koko-ni* A. *kuru sō desu.*
2. *Yagi-san-wa bōeki-no purojekuto-o* B. *takai sō desu.*
3. *Konban shachō-wa Nyū Yōku-ni* C. *taihen da sō desu.*
4. *Senshū totta shashin-ga* D. *iku sō desu.*
5. *Kotoshi-no bōnasu-wa* E. *dekiru sō desu.*
6. *Doitsugo-o jōzu-ni hanasu-no-wa* F. *hanasu sō desu.*
7. *Buchō-wa shigoto-no* G. *shite iru sō desu.*
   ato-de bōnasu-ni tsuite

5. Combine the adjectives with their paired nouns to form the -*sōna* phrase:

ex. rippa, o-tera
➡ *rippasōna o-tera*

hayai, kuruma	*nigiyaka, pātī*
omoshiroi, hon	*wakai, onnanohito*
akarui, e	*muzukashii, tesuto*
samui, tenki	*oishii, kudamono*
sabishii, obā-san	*hazukashii, onnanoko*

JOB LEVELS

gichō
chairperson

shachō
president

fukushachō
vice president

*jōmu torishi-
mariyaku*
executive
director

*senmu
torishi-
mariyaku*
senior
managing
director

buchō
boss of
section chief,
general
manager

jichō
assistant
general
manager

kachō
section chief

shihainin
manager

*fuku
shihainin*
assistant
manager

jūgyōin
employee

SHORT DIALOGUES

1. *ex.* buchō, kachō

Harada: **Buchō**-kara kikimashita-ga
  Sumisu-san-no hanashi-wa yokkatta
  sō desu, ne.
Sumisu: Hontō desu-ka.
Harada: Ē. Shigoto-no ato de dokoka-e
  ikimashō-ka.
Sumisu: Sore-wa ii desu, ne.
Harada: **Kachō**-mo iku-ka kikimashō-ka.
Sumisu: Mochiron. Sō shimashō.

1. shachō, shihainin
2. fuku shihainin, buchō
3. kachō, jichō
4. shachō, kachō

2. *ex.* ie, hiroi, semai

Sumisu: Suwatte-mo ii desu-ka.
Tanaka: Hai, dōzo suwatte kudasai
Sumisu: Tanaka-san-no **ie**-wa totemo ii desu,
  ne. **Hirosōna ie** desu ne.
Tanaka: **Hirosō** desu kedo, jitsu-wa totemo
  semai desu.
Sumisu: Sō desu-ka. Shinjiraremasen, ne.

1. sētā, takai, yasui
2. tēburu, atarashii, furui
3. tsukutta ryōri, taihen, kantan
4. kabin, omoi, karui
5. ryōri, amai, karai

216

3. *ex.* asatte Yamamoto-san-no sōbetsukai-ga aru, ano hoteru-ni iku

Buraun:	Konshū-wa taihen desu ne. Buchō-wa Hara-san-ni kikaku-shitsu-no purojekuto-o tetsudawasete iru sō desu ne.
Hara:	Daijōbu desu, yo. Kyōjū-ni owaru-to omoimasu yo.
Buraun:	Tokorode **asatte Yamamoto-san-no sōbetsukai-ga aru** sō desu ne.
Hara:	Hai. Watashitachi-wa **ano hoteru-ni ikimasu**.
Buraun:	Itsu buchō-wa sono setsumei-o suru-no desu-ka.
Hara:	Hirugohan-no ato de suru sō desu.

1. asatte o-kyaku-san-ga kuru, ano resutoran-ni iku
2. ashita gorufu-o suru, midori-ga oka gorufu kōsu-ni iku
3. raishū kaigi-ga aru, honsha-ni iku
4. raishū-no doyōbi sukī-o suru, Naeba-ni iku

4. *ex.* Morita, yūbe, yaru

> *Buchō: Dareka-ni kono purojekuto-o tetsudatte moraitai-n da ga.*
> *Imai: Boku-ni o-tetsudai sasete kudasai.*
> B: *Isogashii-n ja nai-ka, **Morita**-kun-ga yatte-iru shigoto-no hō-o shite iru-n ja nai-no.*
> I: *Iie, **yūbe** mō katazukemashita.*
> B: *Sō-ka.*
> I: *Hai.*
> B: *Sore nara kore-o **yatte** kureru-kai.*
> I: *Hai. **Yarasete** itadakimasu.*

1. Hara, kesa, suru
2. Watanabe, kinō, kaku
3. Yagi, kyō, katazukeru
4. Tanaka, senshū, keisan suru

SELF-TEST

Fill in the blanks with *wa*, *ga*, *de*, *o*, *ni*, *to*, *no*, *ka*, *ne*, or X:

1. Sensei ___ gakusei ___ iroirona ___ hon ___ yomasemasu.

2. Kachō ___ jūgyōin ___ gorufu ___ ikasemasu.

3. Yamada-san ___ aitai hito ___ Ai Bi Emu ___ tsutomete iru ___ sō desu.

4. Hara-san ___ hoshigatte ___ ita bideo ___ omoshirosō desu.

5. Yagi-san ___ musume ___ akarusōna ___ kodomo desu.

Translate the following sentences into Japanese:

6. With your permission, I will leave early.

7. I understand the chairperson is in the middle of a conference.

8. Please allow me to wait.

9. That is an expensive looking vase.

10. I understand the manager will finish up the project today.

LESSON TWENTY THREE
YŌI-NI NARU DESHŌ

In this lesson you will learn:

- The plain verb + deshō form

- How to state conditional phrases

DIALOGUE

はなぶさ:　とおい ところを ありがとう ございます。

ジョンソン:　どう いたしまして。

はなぶさ:　おまちに なりましたか。

ジョンソン:　いいえ わたしが すこし ばかり はやく きた もの です から カタログを みせて いただきました。すばらしい ですね。

はなぶさ:　ありがとう ございます。

ジョンソン:　わがしゃの あたらしい コンピューター システムに ついて すこし ばかり おはなし させて いただきたいの ですが。よろしい でしょうか。

はなぶさ:　もちろん です。

ジョンソン:　あなたの かいしゃが かいがいへ の しんしゅつを つづける おつもり でしたら この さいしん ぎじゅつの ネットワークが あれば さいこう でしょう。かいがい ししゃと の コミュニケーションが よういに かのう でしょう。

はなぶさ:　そう ですね。わがしゃは すでに きかく しつの ごういを えて にねん いないに とうなん アジアと きた アメリカに しんしゅつ する ことに なって います。

ジョンソン:　もし わがしゃの コンピューター システムを とりいれれば かいがい しんしゅつが よういに なる でしょう。

はなぶさ:　なかなか よさそうな コンピューター システム ですね。

ジョンソン:　カタログを さしあげましょうか。

はなぶさ:　はい ありがとう ございます。

ジョンソン:　おじかんを いただきまして ありがとう ございました。

はなぶさ:　いいえ わざわざ ありがとう ございました。

Hanabusa: *Tōi tokoro-o, arigatō gozaimasu.*

Jonson: *Dō itashimashite.*

H: *O-machi-ni narimashita-ka.*

J: *Iie, watashi-ga sukoshi bakari hayaku kita mono desu kara, katarogu-o misete itadakimashita. Subarashii desu, ne.*

H: *Arigatō gozaimasu.*

J: *Wagasha-no atarashii konpyūtā shisutemu-ni tsuite sukoshi bakari o-hanashi sasete itadakitai-no desu ga. Yoroshii deshō-ka.*

H: *Mochiron desu.*

J: *Anata-no kaisha-ga kaigai-e no shinshutsu-o tsuzukeru o-tsumori deshitara, kono saishin gijutsu-no nettowāku-ga areba saikō deshō. Kaigai shisha-to-no komyunikēshon-ga yōi-ni kanō deshō.*

H: *Sō desu ne. Wagasha-wa sudeni kikaku shitsu-no gōi-o ete, ninen inai-ni Tōnan Ajia to Kita Amerika-ni shinshutsu suru koto-ni natte imasu.*

Hanabusa: You (came) from a far place, thank you.

Johnson: It was nothing.

H: Did you wait for me?

J: No, I came a little early, so I was given the favor of seeing your catalogue. It was excellent.

H: Thank you.

J: I would like the favor of being allowed to speak a little about my company's new computer system. Is that alright?

H: Of course it is.

J: If your company plans to continue expanding overseas, and you had this network, you would have the latest technology. It would enable you to communicate easily (lit. smoothly) with your company's branches.

H: I see. Our corporate planning has already reached a consensus, and it was decided that within the next two years we will expand into Southeast Asia and North America.

"Time is money," is not a popular phrase in Japan. Instead, business people spend a great amount of time with each other in order to develop a friendship and a sense of trust before proceeding to company matters.

221

bakari
just

bengoshi
lawyer

byōki
sick

ete
get...and

gijutsu
technology

gōi
consensus

ima mada
for now

inai-ni
within

kaigai
overseas

kanō(na)
enabled

kaze-o hiku
to catch a
cold

Kita Amerika
North America

**komyuni-
kēshon**
communication

kusuri
medicine

meishi
name or
business card

mitsukeru(-ru)
to find

J: *Moshi wagasha-no
konpyūtā shisutemu-o
toriirereba kaigai
shinshutsu-ga yōi-ni
naru deshō.*

H: *Nakanaka yosasōna
konpyūtā shisutemu
desu, ne.*

J: *Katarogu-o
sashiagemashō-ka.*

H: *Hai, arigatō gozaimasu.*

J: *O-jikan-o itadakimashite,
arigatō gozaimashita.*

H: *Iie, wazawaza arigatō
gozaimashita.*

J: If you used our
computer system,
it would help your
expansion to be very
smooth.

H: That sounds like a
very good computer
system.

J: Shall I leave a
catalogue for you?

H: Yes, thank you.

J: Thank you so much for
your time.

H: No, thank you for all
your trouble.

GRAMMAR EXPLANATION

1. Plain verb + deshō

When a plain verb is added to *deshō*, the
meaning becomes "probably _____."

> ex. *kuru deshō*   probably come
> *kau deshō*   probably buy

> *Zaimu-bu-no hito-wa kaigi-ni **iku deshō**.*
> The people in the finance department will
> probably go to the meeting.

2. -Eba

Verbs

When verbs end in *eba*, they show condition. To
create this verb form, drop the final *u* and add *eba*.

> ex. *toriireru*
> *toriire**eba***   if (you) get and use

miru
mireba   if (you) see
kesu
keseba   if (you) turn it off
magaru
magareba   if (you) turn

For -*u* verbs ending in *tsu*, drop *su* and add *eba*:
  ex. matsu
    mateba   if (you) wait

Ii-no desu often follows these verbs to mean, "If
you _____ it will become good."

  *ex. benkyō sureba **ii-no desu.***
    If (you) study, it will become good, or
    all (you) need to do is study.

    *Anata-wa byōki-no toki, kusuri-o nom**eba***
    ***ii-no desu**.*
    When you get sick, if you take medicine, it
    will become good.

Adjectives

When *i* adjectives end in *kereba*, they show
condition. The meaning becomes "If it is
<u>adj</u>+*kereba*, I will <u>verb</u>." For *i* adjectives, drop the
final *i* and add *kereba*.

  ex. omoshiroi   *omoshiro**kereba***
    takai   *taka**kereba***

  *Eiga-ga omoshiro**kereba**, mimashō.*
  If the movie is interesting, let's see it.
  *Rishi-ga taka**kereba**, okane-o ginkō-ni iremashō.*
  If rates are high, I'll put my money in the bank.

mono desu kara
because

moshi
if

nakanaka
quite good, or (not) easily

nettowāku
network

-ni tsuite
concerning, about

o-machi shimasu
to wait (polite)

pondo
pound

saikō
best

saishin
the latest

shinshutsu
expand

shisha
branch office

shisutemu
system

sōbetsukai
farewell party

sudeni
already

todokeru(-ru)
to deliver

To use *na* adjectives to show condition, add *naraba*

ex. *taihen*
*taihen**naraba***

kirai
*kirai**naraba***

*Boeki purojekuto-ga taihen**naraba**,*
Buchō-ga tetsudatte kudasaru sō desu.
If the trading project is difficult, I understand my boss will help me.

*Kanojo-ga amai tabemono-ga kirai**naraba**,*
keiki-wa agenai hō-ga ii desu.
If she dislikes sweet food, it is better not to give her the cake.

3. -Ra

A final way to show condition is to add *-ra* to a plain past verb.

ex. *datta*
*datta**ra***
*Yamashita-san-ga rusu **dattara** oku-san-ni agete kudasai.*
If Mr. Yamashita is out, please give it to his wife.

kita
*kita**ra***
*Konban Hirakawa-san-ga **kitara**, eiga-o mimashō.*
If Miss Hirakawa comes tonight, let's see the movie.

224

A plain past verb+*ra dō desu-ka* means "how about ___?"

> ex. *Jogingu-o shitara dō desu-ka.*
> How about jogging?
>
> *Kono konpyūtā shisutemu-o kattara dō desu-ka.*
> How about buying this computer system?

EXERCISES

1. -Eba

Answer the questions using the given words:

> ex. *Anata-wa samuku natta toki, dō sureba ii deshō-ka.   sutōbu-o tsukeru*
> ➡ *Sutōbu-o tsukereba ii-no desu.*
>
> *Anata-wa onaka-ga suite iru toki, dō sureba ii deshō-ka.   gohan-o taberu*
>
> *Anata-wa muzukashii tesuto-ga aru toki, dō sureba ii deshō-ka.   benkyō suru*
>
> *Anata-wa kaze-o hiite iru toki, dō sureba ii deshō-ka.   kusuri-o nomu*
>
> *Okane-ga tarinai toki, dō sureba ii deshō-ka. ginkō-de okane-o orosu*
>
> *Anata-wa takushī-o mitsukerarenai toki, dō sureba ii deshō-ka.   basu-ni noru*
>
> *Anata-wa Nihongo-no kotoba-ga wakaranai toki, dō sureba ii deshō-ka.   jisho-o hiku*

Exchanging *meishi* is the first step in developing a business relationship with Japanese people. Be sure to have a generous supply of *meishi* ready when you know that you will be meeting with the Japanese. Have one side printed in English, the other in Japanese. When receiving someone's *meishi*, accept it with both hands, and read it over (even if you do not understand the words). Do not put it away until that person has left the room.

tōgi suru
to discuss

tōi(i)
far

Tōnan Ajia
Southeast
Asia

toriireru(-ru)
to get and use

tsuzukeru
(-ru)
to continue

wagasha
my company

wazawaza
taking so
much trouble

yō
like

yōi(na)
smoothly

yoroshii(i)
polite for yoi

**DEPART-
MENTS**
bu
department

chōsa-bu
business
research

eigyō-bu
sales

gijutsu-bu
engineering

2. -Kereba

Change the adjectives in the first sentence
into the conditional form and combine the two
sentences:

> *ex. Sono tokei-wa takai desu. Tokei-ga kaemasen.*
> ➡ *Sono tokei-ga takakereba kaemasen.*

> *Chūgokugo-wa muzukashii desu.*
> *Chūgokugo-ga benkyō dekimasen.*
> *Sono eiga-wa kowai desu. Sono eiga-o*
> *mitaku arimasen.*
> *Karei-wa karai desu. Karei-o tabetai desu.*
> *Soto-wa atsui desu. Oyogi-ni ikitai desu.*

3. -Ra

Combine the two sentences into one using the
conditional verbs:

> *ex. Okane-ga arimasu. Terebi-o kaimasu.*
> ➡ *Okane-ga attara terebi-o kaimasu.*

> *Nihon-e ikimasu. Yamashita-san-ni aimasu.*
> *En-ga takaku narimasu. Doru-ni ryōgae*
> *shimasu.*
> *Rishi-ga takaku narimasu. Ginkō-ni*
> *futsū yokin shimasu.*
> *Doru-o en-ni ryōgae shimasu. En-de*
> *kaimono dekimasu.*
> *Koko-de machimasu. Iroirona hito-ni aeru*
> *deshō.*

4. Plain verb+deshō

Change the given sentences into the plain verb + *deshō* form:

ex. *Ashita-wa ame-ga takusan furimasu.*
➡ *Ashita-wa ame-ga takusan furu deshō.*

*Kodomo-wa genki-ni narimashita kara,
  ashita gakkō-ni ikimasu.*
*Tonari-ni suwatte iru onnanoko-wa
  Chūgokugo-o hanashimasu.*
*Shujin-wa totemo isogashii node,
  konban ichiji-ni kaerimasu.*
*Asatte Harada-san-wa Tōkyō-ni
  kimasen.*
*Doyōbi-ni buchō-wa gorufu-o
  shimasen.*
*Konban sono purojekuto-o
  katazukemasen.*

**DEPART-
MENTS
(cont.)**

hōki-bu
legal

jinji-bu
personnel

kaigai-bu
international/
overseas

keiri-bu
accounting

kikakushitsu
corporate
planning

kōbai-bu
purchasing

kōhōshitsu
public affairs

māketingu
marketing

rōmu-bu
labor

*seisan-
kanri-bu*
production
control

senden-bu
advertising

*shōhin-
kaihatsu-
shitsu*
product
development

sōmu-bu
general affairs

zaimu-bu
finance

SHORT DIALOGUES

1. *ex.* doru, isoide iru

A: *Watashi-wa **doru**-o en-ni ryōgae shitai
node, ginkō-ni ikanakute-wa ikemasen.*
B: *Demo, kore kara **doru**-ga takaku naru-no
dattara, kyō **doru**-o en-ni ryōgae shinai
hō-ga ii desu yo.*
A: *Iie, kore kara en-ga takaku naru hazu desu.
Ima no hō-ga en-o yasuku kaemasu.*
B: *Sore dewa kyō **doru**-o en-ni ryōgae
suru hō-ga ii desu, ne. Ima **isoide ittara**
sugu ryōgae-ga dekimasu, yo.*
A: *Hai.*

1. pondo, kono densha-ni noru
2. doru, kono kami-ni ki'nyū suru
3. pondo, dekakeru
4. doru, doru-o motte iru

2. *ex.* ashita, gorufu-ni, iku

A: ***Ashita gorufu-ni iku** tsumori desu-ka.*
B: ***Ikitai**-to omoimasu ga iroirona shigoto-o
shinakute-wa ikemasen.*
A: *Kyōjū-ni oeraremasu-ka.*
B: *Yatte mimashō. Hirakawa-san-mo
ikimasu-ka.*
A: *Ē, Hirakawa-san-mo **iku** deshō.*

1. ashita, tenisu-o, suru
2. konban, ongakukai-ni, iku
3. konban, sake-o, nomu

3. *ex.* eigyō, Kita Amerika

> *Buraun: Watashi-wa Ai-Bī-Emu-no Buraun*
> *desu. Meishi-o dōzo.*
> *Hanabusa: Arigatō gozaimasu. Ā, **eigyō**-bu*
> *desu, ne.*
> *Buraun: Ē, sō desu. Kaisha-wa ima **Kita***
> * **Amerika**-ni shinshutsu shite iru sō*
> *desu, ne.*
> *Hanabusa:Ima mada shinshutsu shite imasen*
> *ga, en-ga takaku nareba shinshutsu*
> *suru deshō.*

1. kaigai, Yōroppa
2. kōbai, Tōnan Ajia
3. shōhin-kaihatsu-shitsu, Ōsutoraria
4. zaimu, Amerika
5. seisan-kanri, Furansu
6. mārketingu, Amerika

SELF-TEST

Translate the following sentences into Japanese:

1. The people from the accounting department will probably come to Mr. Yamada's farewell party.

2. If the sashimi is old, it is better not to eat it.

3. If that play is popular, I think we cannot buy a ticket.

4. If my daughter likes that toy, I will buy it.

5. The corporate planning department has reached a consensus, and it was decided that within three years (the company) will expand overseas.

Unscramble the following sentences:

6. jogingu nattara o desu suru tenki ni yotei.

7. deshō ga shinshutsu en nattara e kaigai suru takaku.

8. tsomori wa ni o ni purojekuto desu resutoran kyōjū katazuketara watashitachi iku.

9. ni bōeki yoku deshō gaikoku gaisha tsutomereba ni dekakeru.

10. ga hetanaraba watashi deshō yameru wa Supeingo.

LESSON TWENTY FOUR
O-IWAI SHIMASHŌ

In this lesson you will learn:

- Verb phrases that show respect

- Verb phrases that convey humility

- How to state that a decision has
  been made

DIALOGUE

I

はなぶさ: とうぎを つづけた けっか わがしゃは あなたが
　　　　　ごすいせん くださった システムを つかう ことに
　　　　　きめました。

ジョンソン: ごじんりょく いただきまして ありがとう ございます。
　　　　　これ からも あなたの かいしゃに よい せいひんを
　　　　　ていきょう する ようにどりょく する つもり で
　　　　　おります。

はなぶさ: ありがとう ございます。けいやくしょの なかに
　　　　　しょうらい かえる かも しれない こうもくが にさん
　　　　　あります。でも とうぶん だいじょうぶ です。

ジョンソン: けいかを みながら やって いきましょう。

はなぶさ: わがしゃに とって ただいな とうし ですが
　　　　　おしはらいに ついての しんぱいは ありません。

ジョンソン: それは けっこうな こと です。

はなぶさ: これで せいりつ しましたね。

ジョンソン: こんばん おしょくじに ごしょうたい させて ください。
　　　　　この けいやくの せいりつを おいわい しましょう。

はなぶさ: それは いい ですね。

ジョンソン: ちゅうかりょうりで よろしい ですか。

はなぶさ: はい けっこう です。

II

ジョンソン: かんぱい しましょう。りょうしゃの はってんを
　　　　　いわって。

みんな: かんぱい。

ジョンソン: わたしは あさって ニューヨークに かえりますが
　　　　　また れんらく させて いただきます。

I

Hanabusa: *Tōgi-o tsuzuketa-kekka, wagasha-wa anata-ga go-suisen kudasatta shisutemu-o tsukau koto-ni kimemashita.*

Jonson: *Go-jinryoku itadaki-mashite, arigatō gozaimasu. Kore kara-mo anata-no kaisha-ni yoi seihin-o teikyō suru yō-ni doryoku suru tsumori de orimasu.*

H: *Arigatō gozaimasu. Keiyakusho-no naka-ni shōrai kaeru kamo shirenai kōmoku-ga nisan arimasu. Demo tōbun daijōbu desu.*

J: *Keika-o minagara yatte ikimashō.*

H: *Wagasha-ni totte tadaina tōshi desu ga, o-shiharai-ni tsuite-no shinpai-wa arimasen.*

J: *Sore-wa kekkōna koto desu.*

H: *Kore-de seiritsu shimashita, ne.*

J: *Konban o-shokuji-ni go-shōtai sasete kudasai. Kono keiyaku-no seiritsu-o o-iwai shimashō.*

H: *Sore-wa ii desu, ne.*

I

Hanabusa: After continued discussion, our company has decided to use the (computer) system you recommended.

Johnson: Thank you so much for working hard (to recommend my system). From here I plan to work hard to do a good job of supplying your company.

H: Thank you. There are some contract changes that may need to be made in the future, two or three parts, but for the time being it is all right.

J: Let's do those as we progress.

H: This is a very large investment for our company, but we have no worry concerning raising the funds.

J: That is fine.

H: That is all.

J: Please allow me to invite you (and your colleagues) to dinner this evening to celebrate the conclusion of our contract.

H: That is good.

Greetings are very important in that they set the tone for the entire meeting. Therefore, it is essential that both parties use very respectful, appropriate terms when they first gather together.

chokin
savings

dakyō suru
to compromise

doryoku
doing my best

hatten
prosperity

henkō suru
to change

hitsuyō
need

hodo
approximately

iwatte
here's to

jiki
time

jiki shō sō desu
too soon

jinryoku
doing your best

jōho suru
to concede

kaeru(-ru)
to change

kaiyaku suru
to cancel

kanpai
cheers

J: *Chūkaryōri-de yoroshii desu-ka.*

H: *Hai, kekkō desu.*

II

J: *Kanpai shimashō. Ryōsha-no hatten-o iwatte.*

Minna: *Kanpai.*

J: *Watashi-wa asatte Nyū Yōku-ni kaerimasu ga, mata renraku sasete itadakimasu.*

J: Would Chinese cuisine be good?

H: Yes, that is fine.

II

J: I'd like to propose a toast. Here's to the prosperity of our two companies.

Everyone: Cheers.

J: I will return to New York the day after tomorrow, but I will keep in touch.

GRAMMAR EXPLANATION
1. Go, o-_____-ni naru

To show politeness and respect for another person, use any of the following phrases:

(go) o-verb stem** + *ni narimasu***

ex. *Tanaka-sama-wa konpyūtā shisutemu-o **o-tsukai-ni natte** imasu.*
Mr. Tanaka is using the computer system.

*Dōzo, **o-kake-ni natte** kudasai.*
Please take a seat (honorific).

Exceptions: *suru, iru, iku, kuru, taberu* (see p. 236)

For verbs paired with *suru*, use *go* or *o* + verb + *nasatte*.

ex. **Go-setsumei nasatte** *kudasai.*
Please explain (honorific).

Keiyakusho-o **go-kaiyaku nasatte**
kudasai.
Please cancel the contract (honorific).

Suru, iru, iku, kuru, and *taberu* form completely different words when speaking politely, and do not change into the *-ni naru* form (see p. 236).

-ni naru can be dropped from the *o*-verb-*ni natte kudasai* phrase.

> **o**-verb stem **kudasai**

> ex. **o-kake kudasai**   please take a seat
>   **o-hairi kudasai**   please enter

2. O, go-_____shimasu, itashimasu

This verb phrase shows humility, and in very polite situations should be used to refer to one's self, group or family.

> **o** or **go** verb stem + **shimasu** or ***itashimasu***

> ex. *Watakushi-ga kyasshu kādo-o* **o-mochi shimasu**.
> I hold the money card.

> *Haha-ga* **go-annai shimasu.**
> My mother will show you.

> *Chichi-ga anata-ni* **o-denwa itashimasu**.
> My father will telephone you.

The *o* verb stem-*ni naru kudasai* phrase and *o*-verb stem *kudasai* phrase show higher respect than *-te kudasai.*

Japanese people tend to take a problem solving approach to challenging situations instead of a conquering, win or lose approach. This stems from their being forced to cooperate with the harsh nature conditions exisiting in their islands. They have endured countless natural disaters and therefore look for ways to accommodate difficult circumstances.

keika
progress

keiyakusho
contract
document

-kekka
as a result of

kimeru(-ru)
to decide

kōmoku
sections,
parts

kōshin suru
to renew

kyōmi-ga aru
to be
interested in

miokuru
to let go of

moshi moshi
hello
(telephone)

-ni totte
for

nisan
two or three

renraku
keep in touch

ryōsha
two companies

seiritsu suru
to conclude

(o)shiharai
funds

shihon
capital

3. -Koto-ni kimeru

To say that one has made a decision, add the
-koto-ni kimeru phrase to the plain verb.

ex. Anata-ga go-suisen kudasatta kikai-o
tsukau **koto-ni kimemashita**.
We have decided to use the machine that
you did the favor of recommending to us.

Tōbun-wa anata-no kaisha keiyakusho-o
kōshin shinai **koto-ni kimemashita**.
For the time being, we have decided not
to renew the contract with your company.

EXERCISES
1. Humble/honorific verbs

These should be used in very formal situations:

	Humble	Honorific
suru	itashimasu	nasaimasu
iru	orimasu	irasshaimasu
iku	mairimasu	irasshaimasu
kuru	mairimasu	irasshaimasu
taberu	itadakimasu	meshiagarimasu

2. O-____ni naru

Change the following sentences into the o-verb-ni
natte kudasai form:

ex. Keiyakusho-o yomu
➡ Keiyakusho-o o-yomi-ni natte kudasai.

tegami-o kaku ryōri-o tsukuru
kippu-o kau ie-ni kaeru

jisho-o hiku   tōshi-ni tsuite kimeru

atarashii konpyūtā shisutemu-o tsukau

3. O-verb stem + suru, itasu

Convert the following phrases into the o-verb stem *suru, itasu* form:

ex. yomu

Gakusei: O-**yomi** shimashō-ka.

Sensei: Hai, **yonde** kudasai.

karimasu	matsu	motsu
toru	watasu	okuru
harau	yomu	toru

4. -Koto-ni kimeru

Change the following sentence to reflect that a decision was made:

ex. Watashi-wa genkin go man en-o oroshimasu.

➡ *Watashi-wa genkin go man en-o orosu koto-ni kimemashita.*

Watashi-wa en-o doru-ni ryōgae shimasen.

Watashi-wa Buraun-san-ga kaitagatte ita saifu-o kare-ni agemasu.

Yūbe karita hon-o modoshimasu.

Shigoto-no ato de Tanaka-san-no sukina resutoran-ni ikimasu.

Kaigi chū-ni suraido-o miseru.

Kore kara jichō-wa bōnasu-o keisan shimasu.

Kaisha-wa Kita Amerika-ni shinshutsu shimasu.

-Kekka
Kekka is a suffix added to plain past verbs; it means "as a result of." ex. *Tōgi shita-kekka, watashitachi-wa atarashii komyunikēshon shisutemu-o suisen shimasu.* As a result of our discussions, we recommend the new communication system.

shikin
funds

shinpai
worry

shisan
assets

shō shō
o-machi
kudasai
just a moment
(very polite)

shōrai
future

shōtai suru
to invite

shūsei suru
to correct

suisen suru
to recommend

tadai(na)
huge

teikyō
supply/service

tōbun
for the time
being

tōshi
investment

yoroshii(i)
good (polite)

yoyaku
reservation

yoyū
afford

SHORT DIALOGUES

1. *ex.* seihin, motsu

A: O-jikan-o itadakimashite, arigatō
gozaimashita.

B: Dō itashimashite. Wagasha-wa anata-no
go-suisen kudasatta **seihin**-o kau koto-ni
kimemashita.

A: Go-jinryoku itadakimashite, arigatō
gozaimasu. Itsu anata-no kaisha-ni
seihin-o o-mochi shimashō-ka.

B: Raishū-no kayōbi-ni o-**mochi**
kudasai.

A: Hai, wakarimashita.

1. konpyūtā, todokeru
2. kikai, todokeru
3. komyunikēshon shisutemu, motsu
4. seihin, todokeru

2. *ex.* kōhī, seihin-o tsukau, jiki shō sō desu

A: Dōzo, o-kake-ni natte kudasai. **Kōhī**-o
ikaga desu-ka.

B: Hai, arigatō gozaimasu.

A: Dōzo, meshiagatte kudasai.

B: Itadakimasu. Anata-no kaisha-wa wagasha-
no **seihin-o tsukau** koto-ni narimashita-ka.

A: Sō desu ne. Tōgi-o tsuzuketakekka,
ima-wa **jiki shō sō desu** node,
miokuru koto-ni kimemashita.

B: Wakarimashita. Dewa, mata renraku-o
sasete itadakimasu. Shōrai nanika o-
tetsudai dekiru koto-ga arimashitara,
oshirase kudasai.

A: Arigatō gozaimasu.

1. ocha, konpyūtā-o tsukau, taihenna jiki desu
2. kōcha, kikai-o kau, mada kyōmi-ga arimasen
3. kōhi, seihin-o kau, mada yoyū-ga arimasen
4. kōcha, shisutemu-o toriireru, mada hitsuyō arimasen

3. *ex.* denwa chū desu, juppun

Sumisu:	Moshi moshi, Ai Bī Emu-no Sumisu desu.
Hara:	Konnichi-wa.
Sumisu:	Konnichi-wa. Tanaka-sama-wa irasshaimasu-ka.
Hara:	Shō shō o-machi kudasai.
Sumisu:	Hai.
Hara:	Moshi moshi. Sumimasen ga, Tanaka-wa ima **denwa chū desu.**
Sumisu:	Sore dewa, **juppun** hodo shitara mata denwa-o itashimashō-ka.
Hara:	Hai, onegai shimasu.
Sumisu:	Jā, mata.

1. kaigi chū de gozaimasu, ichijikan
2. orimasen demo sugu-ni mairimasu, sanjuppun
3. kaisha-ni orimasen, yonjuppun
4. sukoshi isogashii desu demo sugu-ni hima-ni naru deshō, jūgofun

When "yes" may mean "no"
Japanese people do not like to disagree or contradict someone directly. If you notice hesitation before they say "yes," they may be saying "yes I understand" but it doesn't mean they agree with you. Stop and ask *Taihen desu-ka*. If they agree that it's difficult, then the "yes" probably meant "no."

If you cannot close a sale or reach an agreement with a Japanese company, try to bow out gracefully, being careful not to humiliate them or embarrass yourself. They may be impressed with your attitude and want to work with you in the future.

SELF-TEST

Translate the following sentences into Japanese:

1. Our corporate planning department has reached a consensus, and we have decided to renew the contract.

2. Please use the computer (honorific).

3. Please buy a picture at that store (honorific).

4. My father will show you the post office (humble).

5. My older sister will call her boss (humble).

6. We have decided to go to Europe next month.

7. After continued discussion, my company has decided to expand overseas.

8. Please allow me to keep in touch.

9. I'd like to propose a toast.

10. Thank you for trying your best.

LESSON TWENTY FIVE
ATAMA-GA ITAI DESU

In this lesson you will learn:

- The parts of the body

- Expressing pain

- The -tame ni phrase

- Another -reru, -rareru verb form

DIALOGUE

I

A: どう しましたか。いたそう ですね。

B: でんしゃの ドアに ゆびを はさまれて しまいました。
レントゲンを とる ために びょういんへ いかなければ
なりません。

A: ああ これは ひどい ですね。とても いたみますか。

B: すこし よく なりましたが レントゲンを とった ほうが
いいと おもいます。それに ともだちに かぜを うつされて
しまいました。

A: なにか わたしに できる ことが あったら おしえて ください。

B: ありがとう ございます。

II

いしゃ: こっせつは して いない ので しんぱいは ありません。

B: ああ よかった。

いしゃ: アスピリンを のんだら いたみは おさまる でしょう
でも もし まだ いたかったら また きて ください。
しょほうせんを かきましょう。

B: ありがとう ございます。

いしゃ: アスピリンは ねつにも ききます。にさん にち
やすめば よく なる でしょう。

B: ありがとう ございます。

I

A: *Dō shimashita-ka. Itasō desu, ne.*

B: *Densha-no doa-ni yubi-o hasamarete shimaimashita. Rentogen-o toru tame-ni byōin-e ikanakereba narimasen.*

I

A: What's wrong? You look like you are in pain.

B: The train door was shut on my fingers. I have to go to the hospital in order to get an x-ray taken.

A: *Ā, kore-wa hidoi desu, ne. Totemo itamimasu-ka.*

B: *Sukoshi yoku narimashita ga, rentogen-o totta hō-ga ii-to omoimasu. Sore ni tomodachi-ni kaze-o utsusarete shimaimashita.*

A: *Nanika watashi-ni dekiru koto-ga attara oshiete kudasai.*

B: *Arigatō gozaimasu.*

II

Isha: *Kossetsu-wa shite inai node, shinpai-wa arimasen.*

B: *Ā, yokatta.*

I: *Asupirin-o nondara, itami-wa osamaru deshō, demo moshi mada itakattara mata kite kudasai. Shohōsen-o kakimashō.*

B: *Arigatō gozaimasu.*

I: *Asupirin-wa netsu-ni-mo kikimasu. Nisan nichi yasumeba yoku naru deshō.*

B: *Arigatō gozaimasu.*

A: Oh, that's terrible. Does it hurt a lot?

B: It is a little better, but I think I should still get an x-ray. Besides that, my friend passed her cold to me.

A: If there is something I can do, please let me know.

B: Thank you.

II

Doctor: Nothing is broken, so there is nothing to worry about.

B: Oh, that's good.

D: If you take aspirin, it will ease the pain, but if you still have pain, please come back. I can write a prescription.

B: Thank you.

D: The aspirin will also help your fever. You should be better if you rest for two or three days.

B: Thank you.

Very few private doctor offices exist in Japan. Most people receive health care at a hospital, regardless of the severity of the illness.

243

hasamaru(-u)
to pinch

hidoi(i)
terrible

itami
pain

itamu(-u)
to feel pain

kiku(-u)
to have an
effect

kossetsu
broken

kōun
lucky, fortunate

nyūin suru
admitted to a
hospital

omimai
visit one in
the hospital

osaeru
to ease
(needs object)

osamaru(-u)
to ease (no
object)

shinu(-u)
to die

sore-ni
besides that

tame-ni
in order to

**-te shimai-
mashita**
completely +
verb

GRAMMAR EXPLANATION

1. Expressing Pain

When a part of your body aches or hurts, the sentence to use is as follows:

Body part-*ga itai desu.*

ex. Nodo-*ga itai desu.*
I have a sore throat.

Onaka-*ga itai desu.*
I have a stomach ache.

2. Tame-ni

This phrase is used to describe why a certain action takes place. The sentence structure is:

Goal *tame-ni* what one does

Obj. + plain verb **tame-ni** object, verb

ex. Genki-ni naru **tame-ni** kusuri-o nomimasu.
Take medicine in order to get better.

Nihongo-o benkyō suru **tame-ni** Nihon-ni ikimasu.
Go to Japan in order to study Japanese.

3. -Reru, -rareru

This verb form means that one has suffered as a result of another's actions. To form this pattern, use the *nai* verb form. Drop the final *nai* and add *reru* for *-u* verbs and *rareru* for *-ru* verbs.

> *ex. yamenai   yamerareru*
> *yaranai   yarareru*
> *hasamanai   hasamareru*

> Exceptions: *shinai   sareru*
> *kuru   korareru*

Sentence Structure:

> Sufferer+***wa*** thing inflicting suffering-***ni reru***,
> ***rareru*** verb

> *ex. Watashi-wa ame-**ni furaremashita**.*
> It rained on me.

> *Honda-no kaisha-**ni** kaigi-o kyanseru*
> ***saremashita**.*
> Honda cancelled the meeting on me.

EXERCISES

1. Memorize the body parts:

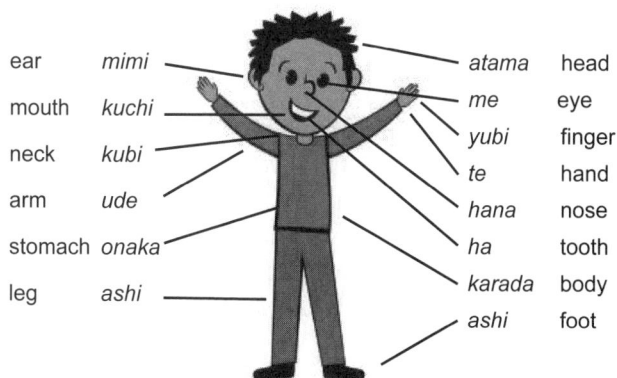

ear	*mimi*		*atama*	head
mouth	*kuchi*		*me*	eye
neck	*kubi*		*yubi*	finger
arm	*ude*		*te*	hand
stomach	*onaka*		*hana*	nose
leg	*ashi*		*ha*	tooth
			karada	body
			ashi	foot

Shimasu
In English, when talking about medical care, we usually use "had" when referring to things that have been done to us. *ex.* I had an operation, I had a shot, etc. However in Japanese, the word *shimasu* is used. *ex. Shujutsu-o **shimashita**.* Lit: An operation was done. *Kenkō shindan-o **shimashita**.* I had a physical examination, or a physical examination was done.

**utsuru(-u),
utsusu(-u)**
to infect

yasumu(-u)
to take a rest

**TYPES OF
ILLNESS
arerugī**
allergy

gan
cancer

haien
pneumonia

ikaiyō
ulcer

kōketsuatsu
high blood
pressure

mōchōen
appendicitis

netsu
fever

shinzōbyō
heart disease

teiketsuatsu
low blood
pressure

**PHARMACY
asupirin**
aspirin

kazegusuri
cold medicine

megusuri
eye drops

seki dome
cough
suppressant

Using the body parts just learned, state that a specific part hurts:

_____-ga itai desu.

ex. **Atama**-ga itai desu.

2. -Tame-ni

Combine the given sentences using the tame-ni phrase:

ex. Itami-o osaetai desu. Desu kara,
    asupirin-o nomimasu.
➡ Itami-o osaeru tame-ni asuprin-o
    nomimasu.

Genki-ni naritai desu. Desu kara,
    shujutsu-o shimasu.
Nihon-ni ikitai desu. Desu kara,
    arubaito-o shimasu.
Kangofu-ni naritai desu. Desu kara,
    kagaku-o benkyō shimasu.
Kōza-o hirakitai desu. Desu kara,
    ginkō-ni ikimasu.
Hara-san-no tanjōbi-no pātī-no
    okurimono-o kaitai desu. Desu
    kara, genkin-o oroshimasu.

3. -Reru, -rareru

Change the phrases into the -reru, -rareru form:

ex. Kodomo-ga kaze-o hikimashita.
➡ Kodomo-ni kaze-o hikaremashita.

246

*Toyota-no kaisha-ga keiyakusho-no
kōmoku-o kaemashita.*
Buchō-ga kaigi-o kyanseru shimashita.
*O-kyaku-san-ga keiyakusho-no
kōmoku-o kaemashita.*
*Tomodachi-ga kuruma-no doa-de
yubi-o hasamimashita.*
*Chichi-ga watashi-no teiki yokin-kara
genkin-o hikidashimashita.*
Jūgyōin-ga kyū-ni yamemashita.
Isogashii toki-ni tomodachi-ga kimashita.
Haha-ga shinimashita.

SHORT DIALOGUES

1. *ex.* kodomotachi, kaze-o, utsusu

A: *Dō shimashita-ka.*
B: *Kinō* **kodomotachi**-*ni* **kaze-o
utsusarete** *shimaimashita.*
A: *Ā, kore-wa hidoi desu, ne.*
B: *Ē, sore-ni konban shujin-no kaisha-no
hito-ni pātī-ni shōtai sarete iru node,
dekakenakute-wa ikemasen.*
A: *Taihen desu, ne.*
   1. densha-no doa, ashi-o, hasamu
   2. tomodachi, kaze-o, utsusu
   3. kuruma-no doa, yubi-o, hasamu
   4. o-isha-san, chūsha-o, suru

AT THE HOSPITAL

chūsha
shot, injection

do
degrees
(centigrade)

haisha-san
dentist

kangofu-san
nurse

kenkō shindan
physical examination

kibun
feeling

hakike
nausea

(o)isha-(san)
doctor

itai
pain, hurt

rentogen
x-ray

shohōsen
prescription

shujutsu
operation

taion
body temperature

2. *ex.* Doitsugo, Doitsu

A: *Nani-o shite iru-no desu-ka.*
B: ***Doitsugo**-o jōzu-ni hanasu tame-ni benkyō shite imasu.*
A: *Ā, sore-wa ii desu, ne.* ***Doitsu**-ni itta koto-ga arimasu-ka.*
B: *Mada arimasen.*
A: *Jā,* ***Doitsugo**-ga jōzu-ni hanasu yō-ni nattara, soko-ni iku tsumori desu-ka.*
B: *Ē,* ***Doitsu**-ni iku yotei desu.*

1. Furansugo, Furansu
2. Eigo, Ōsutoraria
3. Chūgokugo, Chūgoku
4. Eigo, Igirisu

3. *ex.* fuku-shachō, ikaiyō

A: *Sakki hidoi koto-o kikimashita.*
B: *Nandesu-ka.*
A: ***Fuku-shachō**-wa hidoi **ikaiyō** da sō desu ne.*
B: *Shinjiraremasen, ne. Ima **fuku-shachō**-wa byōin-ni iru-no desu-ka.*
A: *Ē, Yūbe nyūin shimashita.*
B: *Shujutsu-o suru-no desu-ka.*
A: *Ē, sugu-ni shujutsu-o suru sō desu, ne.*
B: *Jā, isshoni omimai-ni ikimashō.*

1. senmu, gan
2. jichō, shinzōbyō
3. jōmu, mōchōen
4. kachō, ikaiyō

SELF-TEST

Unscramble the following sentences:

1. ni o toru tame byōin ni rentogen ikimasu.

2. naru ni genki shimasu ni o tame chūsha.

3. Toyota ni o kaisha kyanseru saremashita no kaigi.

4. doa no ashi shimaimashita o hasamarete ni basu.

5. ga itai node nomimasu kusuri o nodo.

Fill in the blanks with wa, ga, de, o, ni, to, no, ka, ne, or X:

6. Ude ___ totemo itai ___ desu. Desu kara, byōin ___ rentogen ___ torimasu.

7. Kusuri ___ kau ___ tame ___ yakkyoku ___ ikimasu.

8. Senshū ___ tomodachi ___ kaze ___ utsusarete ___ shimaimashita.

9. Hara-san ___ kodomo ___ kaze ___ utsusarete ___ shimaimashita.

10. Yoku miru ___ tame ___ megane ___ kakemasu.

SELF-TEST ANSWERS

Lesson 1
1. Sumimasen, ima nanji desu-ka.
2. Pātī-wa rokuji kara jūichiji made desu.
3. Arigatō gozaimasu.
4. Watashi-no denwa bangō-wa ni go ich no kyū roku yon san desu.
5. Ima gozen jūniji-han desu.
6. Tōkyō-wa nanji desu-ka.
7. Tōkyō-wa ima asa desu.
8. Tōkyō-wa ima yoru desu.
9. Gogo sanji desu-ka.
10. Sō desu.

Lesson 2
1. Kinō-wa getsuyōbi deshita.
2. Are-wa ikura desu-ka.
3. Ano shatsu-wa ikura desu-ka.
4. Kono wanpīsu-wa takai desu.
5. Ima sangatsu desu.
6. Kono kōto-o kudasai.
7. Are-wa ikura desu-ka.
8. Sono nekutai-wa yasui desu ne.
9. Kyō-wa nanyōbi desu-ka.
10. Sono bōshi-o kudasai.

Lesson 3
1. Enpitsu wa kaban no naka ni arimasu.
2. Anata no hon wa tēburu no ue ni arimasu ka.
3. Michiko san wa kuruma no mae ni imasu.
4. Emiko san wa doko desu ka.
5. Isu wa tēburu no ushiro ni arimasu.
6. Jonson-san-no nōto-wa tsukue-no naka-ni arimasu.
7. Watashi-no pen-wa doko-ni arimasu-ka.
8. Kami-wa tsukue-no shita-ni arimasu.
9. Hara-san-no kutsu-wa doko-ni arimasu-ka.
10. Jonson-san-wa resutoran-ni imasu.

Lesson 4
1. Jonson san wa sushi o tabemashita.
2. Watashi wa mizu o nomimashita.
3. Michiko san wa Tōkyō ni kimashita.

4. Watashi <u>wa</u> Nihongo <u>o</u> benkyō shimasu.
5. Kinō, Jonson <u>san</u> <u>wa</u> terebi <u>o</u> mimashita <u>ka</u>.
6. Kyō, watashi-wa Eigo-o oshiemasu.
7. Kinō, Michiko-san-wa Amerika-ni kimashita.
8. Sumisu-san-wa hashirimasu-ka.
9. Watashi-wa hon-o yomimashita.
10. Watashi-wa Nihongo-o hanashimasu.

Lesson 5
1. Kochira-wa Michiko-san-no obā-san desu.
2. Hajimemashite.
3. Dōzo, yoroshiku.
4. Anata-no namae-wa nandesu-ka.
5. Kyō kare-no otō-san-wa Eigo-o benkyō shimasen.
6. Mitsumura-san-no imōto-san-wa sushi-o tabemasen.
7. Kinō, Tanaka-san-no onii-san-wa hon-o yomimashita.
8. Watashi-no namae-wa Jonson desu.
9. Anata-no oba-san-no hon-wa tsukue-no naka-ni arimasen.
10. Kinō, watashi-wa tomadachi-ni aimashita.

Lesson 6
1. Nemashō.
2. Eigakan-ni ikimashō.
3. Watashi-wa byōin-ni ikimasen deshita.
4. Anata-wa ocha-o nomimasen deshita-ka.
5. Watashi-wa aoi kuruma-o unten shimasen deshita.
6. Watashi-wa murasaki iro-no tsukue-o mimasu.
7. Anata-wa biyōin-ni ikimashita-ka.
8. Ano onnanohito-wa akai hon-o yomimasu.
9. Ano shiroi tatemono-wa ginkō desu.
10. Kare-wa resutoran-ni imasu.

Lesson 7
1. Kuruma <u>wa</u> kiiro <u>kute</u> chiisai desu.
2. Akai budōshu <u>wa</u> arimasu <u>ka</u>.
3. Asoko <u>de</u> gohan <u>o</u> tabemashita.
4. Tanaka <u>san</u> <u>no</u> ie <u>de</u> yasashii hon <u>o</u> yomimashita.
5. Sumisu <u>san</u> <u>wa</u> <u>o</u> sashami <u>ga</u> suki desu <u>ka</u>.
6. Sore-wa kirei-de takai desu.
7. Karashi-wa oishii desu-ka.
8. Shiroi budōshu-wa amari suki dewa arimasen.
9. Gakkō-de Nihongo-o benkyō

shimasen deshita.
10. Tōkyō-ga daisuki desu.

Lesson 8

1. Oji san wa eigakan de eiga o mite imasu.
2. Onii san wa ginkō de matte imasu.
3. Keigo san to Masāki san wa sakkā o shite imasu.
4. Ame ga futte imasu.
5. Michiko san wa doko de ocha o nonde imasu ka.
6. Kanojo-wa akakute hayai kuruma-o unten shite imasu.
7. Kare-wa oishii ringo-o tabete imasu.
8. Watashi-wa Nihongo-o naratte imasu.
9. Michiko-san-wa Eigo-o benkyō shite imasen.
10. Watashi-wa depāto-de iroirona hito-ni aimashita.

Lesson 9

1. Tenpura-o tabete kudasai.
2. Niji jūgofun gurai uchi-ni kite kudasai.
3. Ginkō-wa dochira desu-ka.
4. Kippu-o katte kudasai.
5. Nisen en tarimasen.
6. Obā-san-wa o-genki desu-ka.
7. Goji sanjūkyūfun made matte kudasai.

8. Komakai okane-o motte imasu-ka.
9. Anata-wa mainichi shigoto-ni itte imasu-ka.
10. Kochira-ni kite kudasai.

Lesson 10

1. Maiasa X Nihongo o benkyō shite imasu.
2. Isshūkan ni san do resutoran de tabemasu.
3. Watashi wa ikkagetsukan ni ikkai Kyōto ni ikimasu.
4. Senshū no kinyōbi no tesuto wa muzukashikatta X desu.
5. Raishū no mokuyōbi ni shigoto o hajimemasu.
6. Kinyōbi-wa yasumi dewa arimasen.
7. Isshūkan-ni ichi-do depāto-ni ikimasu.
8. Kyō-wa jūnigatsu itsuka desu.
9. Kinyōbi-ni muzukashii tesuto-o ukemashita.
10. Tanaka-san-to issho-ni hirugohan-o tabemashita.

Lesson 11

1. Raishū-no mokuyōbi-ni Kyōto-ni ikitai desu.
2. Watashi-wa ishhūkan-ni sankai Nihongo-o benkyō shitai desu.
3. Hayaku kite kudasai.

4. Kare-wa watashi-no senpai kamo shiremasen.
5. Tanaka-san-wa eigakan-ni ikanai kamo shiremasen.
6. Kyō-wa amari samuku arimasen.
7. Ojii-san-wa genki dewa arimasen.
8. Konban anata-wa kurashikku-no ongakukai-ni ikimasen-ka.
9. Sono eiga-wa omoshiroku arimasen deshita.
10. Watashi-wa Fuji ginkō-ni tsutometai desu.

Lesson 12

1. Nihon-to Ōsutoraria dewa dochira no hō-ga hiroi desu-ka.
2. Kono kissaten-wa totemo konde imasu ne.
3. Ano tatemono-ga ichiban takai desu.
4. Motto ōkina sētā-ga hoshii desu.
5. Hiragana yori-mo kantan desu.
6. Kono ningyō wa hoka no ningyō X yori mo takai desu.
7. Sono eiga to ano eiga wa dochira no hō ga omoshiroi desu ka.
8. Kono saizu no hō ga ōkii X desu.

9. Watashi wa motto X ōkina sētā o kaitai desu.
10. Motto X akarui iro no mono ga arimasu ka.

Lesson 13

1. Mori-san-wa shinrigaku-no hon-o yonda-to omoimasu.
2. Kare-wa kōgaku-o benkyō shita-to omoimashita.
3. Watashi-no ushiro-ni suwatte iru onnanohito-wa gohan-o tabete imasu.
4. Hon-o yonde iru otokonohito-wa Jonson-san desu.
5. Kuruma-o unten shite iru onnanohito-wa Tōkyō-no kata desu.
6. Isshukan ni ikkai X shinrigaku no kyōshitsu ni ikimasu.
7. Sushi o tabete iru X hito wa sensei ni naru to omoimasu.
8. Yamada-san no ushiro ni suwatte iru X hito wa Mori-san desu.
9. Megane o kakete iru X hito wa sensei desu.
10. Tanaka-san wa daigaku de iroirona supōtsu o shita to omoimasu.

Lesson 14

1. Anata-wa Nihongo-no zasshi-o yonda koto-ga

arimasu-ka.
2. Anata-wa Naomi-san-ni atta koto-ga arimasu-ka.
3. Sono daibutsu-wa rippa desu.
4. Kio tsukete kudasai.
5. Akachan-wa aruite iru-no desu.
6. Donna chizu desu-ka.
7. Kare-wa sukī-o shite iru-no desu.
8. Konna sumāto fon-o tsukatta koto-ga arimasu-ka.
9. Kanojo-wa gakui-o torimashita.
10. Kanji-wa hiragana-yori-mo muzukashii desu.

Lesson 15
1. Daigaku ni ita toki rekishi o benkyō shimashita.
2. Tanaka san wa shigoto no ato de sake o nomitai to iimashita.
3. Ano hito wa jogingu o shinagara iyahōn o shite imasu.
4. Yamada san wa zasshi ga zenzen nai to iimashita.
5. Hara san wa tachinagara hanashi o shite imasu.
6. Toyota ni tsutomete ita X toki X iroirona sheihin o shōkai shimashita.
7. Harada-san wa 「anata wa

kono hon o yonda ka 」–to kikimashita.
8. Yamada-san no tsukutta X gohan wa totemo X oishikatta desu.
9. Watashitachi ga kinō X mita bideo wa sugokatta-n desu X.
10. Hara-san wa 「anata ga katta sētā wa kirei da」 to iimashita.

Lesson 16
1. Sono akachan-wa jibun-de arukemasu.
2. Obā-san-wa Eigo-ga hanasemasu.
3. Hara-san-wa tenisu-ga dekimasu.
4. Tenki-wa samuku natte imasu.
5. Yonin-de suwaremasu.
6. Natsu yasumi watashi-wa Sapporo-ni iku koto-ga dekimasu.
7. Tanaka-san-wa sukī-ga jōzu-ni natte imasu.
8. Hitori-de uchi-ni koraremasu-ka.
9. Kekkon shiki-wa subarashikatta-to omoimasu.
10. Futari-wa gakkō-de o-bentō-o tabeta-no desu.

Lesson 17

1. Yūbe, okurimono-o kawanakatta.
2. Hora. *or* Hai dōzo.
3. Jikan-ga nakatta-no desu.
4. Watashi-wa o-tera-ni ikitaku nai-to omoimasu.
5. Hara-sama-wa Honda-ni tsutomete irasshaimasu-ka.
6. Kono shūmatsu sukī-o shitaku arimasen.
7. Watashi-wa Tōkyō-ni sunde orimasu.
8. Sono kūkō-wa ōkiku nakatta.
9. Nihon-no zasshi-wa Amerika-no zasshi-to chigaimasu.
10. Ashlta, Ōsutoraria-ni iku tsumori desu.

Lesson 18

1. Chichi-ga kono tokei-o kuremashita.
2. Otōto-ni tokei-o moraimashita.
3. Sensei-ga jisho-o kudasaimashita.
4. Sensei-ni pen-o itadakimashita.
5. Haha-wa Amerika-ni sunde orimasu.
6. Ojama shimashita.
7. Dōzo, okamainaku.
8. Imōto-wa jūyon-sai desu.
9. Ani-wa Nihon-ni kitagatte iru-to omoimasu.
10. Morita sensei-wa chichi-no ie-ni irasshaimashita.

Lesson 19

1. Sensei-ga hanashi-o kakuno-o tetsudatte kudasaimashita.
2. Watashi-wa Matsumoto-san-ni yūbinkyoku-ni tsurete itte itadakimashita.
3. Watashi-wa Morimoto sensei-ni shōsetsu-o sashiagemashita.
4. Watashi-wa imōto-ni Nihongo-no hon-o agemashita.
5. Morita-san-ni kono hagaki-o okutte hoshii desu.
6. Watashi <u>wa</u> haha <u>ni</u> bideo <u>o</u> agemashita.
7. Watashi <u>wa</u> sensei <u>ni</u> jisho <u>o</u> sashiagemashita.
8. Chichi <u>ga</u> watashi <u>ni</u> hon <u>o</u> katte <u>X</u> kuremashita.
9. Anata <u>ni</u> kore <u>o</u> mite <u>X</u> hoshii desu.
10. Kyō <u>X</u> Mitsutake-san <u>wa</u> koko <u>ni</u> kuru to omoimasu.

Lesson 20

1. Ano kado de magaranaide kudasai.
2. Basu-wa sanji-ni koko-de tomaru hazu desu.

3. Anata-no (ga) tsukutta gohan-o tabete-mo ii desu-ka.

4. Asatte, watashi-wa sukī-o shite tenisu-o suru tsumori desu.

5. Kono kado-o migi-ni magatte-wa ikemasen.

6. Kono kōsaten-no temae-de yū tān shite-mo ii desu-ka.

7. Densha-de Kyōto-ni itte-mo ii desu-ka.

8. Kyō watashi-wa shigoto-o hachiji-ni oeru tsumori desu.

9. Untenshu-san, kochiragawa de tomaranaide kudasai.

10. Tōkyō-ni itte, tokei-o kaimasu.

Lesson 21

1. Kyō-wa shinbun-o yondari sushi-o tsukuttari shite imasu.

2. Genkin-o hikidasu-ni-wa, kono kyasshu kādo-o tsukawanakute-wa ikemasen.

3. Haha-no okurimono-o kawanakute-wa ikemasen.

4. Yonjuppēji made yomanakute-wa ikemasen.

5. En-o doru-ni ryōgae shite kudasai.

6. Morita-san-ga suki datta resutoran-ni itte mimashō.

7. Shujin-no tsukutta gohan-o tabete mimashō.

8. Akachan-wa tabetari, nemuttari shite imasu.

9. Atsuku narimashita kara mado-o akenakereba narimasen.

10. Kōza-o hirakanakereba narimasen.

Lesson 22

1. Sensei wa gakusei ni iroirona X hon o yomasemasu.

2. Kachō wa jūgyōin ni gorufu ni ikasemasu.

3. Yamada-san ga aitai hito wa Ai Bi Emu ni tsutomete iru X sō desu.

4. Hara-san no hoshigatte X ita bideo wa omoshirosō desu.

5. Yagi-san no musume wa akarusōna X kodomo desu.

6. Hayaku kaerasete kudasai.

7. Kaichō-wa kaigi chū da sō desu.

8. Matasete kudasai.

9. Sore-wa takasōna kabin desu.

10. Shihainin-wa purojekuto-o kyōjū-ni katazukeru sō desu.

Lesson 23

1. Tabun keiri-bu-no hitotachi-wa Yamada-san-no sōbetsukai-ni kuru deshō.

2. O-sashimi-wa furukereba,

tabenai hō-ga ii-no desu.

3. Moshi sono geki-ga ninki-ga attara, kippu-wa kaenai-to omoimasu.

4. Musume-ga sono omocha-o sukinaraba, sore-o kaimasu.

5. Kikaku-shitsu-no gōi-o ete, sannen inai-ni kaigai-ni shinshutsu suru koto-ni natte imasu.

6. Tenki-ni nattara jogingu-o suru yotei desu.

7. En-ga takaku nattara, kaigai-e shinshutsu suru deshō.

8. Watashitachi-wa purojekuto-o kyōjū-ni katazuketara, resutoran-ni iku tsumori desu.

9. Bōeki gaisha-ni tsutomereba, yoku gaikoku-ni dekakeru deshō.

10. Watashi-wa Supeingo-ga hetanaraba, yameru deshō.

Lesson 24

1. Kikaku-shitsu-no gōi-o ete, keiyakusho-o kōshin suru koto-ni kimemashita.

2. Konpyūtā-o o-tsukai-ni natte kudasai.

3. Ano mise-de e-o o-kai-ni natte kudasai.

4. Chichi-ga yūbinkyoku-o go-annai shimasu.

5. Ane-ga buchō-ni o-denwa

itashimasu.

6. Raigetsu Yōroppa-ni iku koto-ni kimemashita.

7. Tōgi-o tsuzuketa-kekka, wagasha-wa kaigai-ni shinshutsu suru koto-ni kimemashita.

8. Renraku sasete itadakimasu.

9. Kanpai shimashō.

10. Go-jinryoku itadakimashite, arigatō gozaimasu.

Lesson 25

1. Rentogen-o toru tame-ni byōin-ni ikimasu.

2. Genki-ni naru tame-ni chūsha-o shimasu.

3. Toyota-no kaisha-ni kaigi-o kyanseru saremashita.

4. Basu-no doa-ni ashi-o hasamarete shimaimashita.

5. Nodo-ga itai node, kusuri-o nomimasu.

6. Ude ga totemo itai X desu. Desu kara, byōin de rentogen o torimasu.

7. Kusuri o kau X tame ni yakkyoku ni ikimasu.

8. Senshū X tomodachi ni kaze o utsusarete X shimaimashita.

9. Hara-san no kodomo ni kaze o utsusarete X shimaimashita.

10. Yoku miru X tame ni megane o kakemasu.

JAPANESE-ENGLISH INDEX

ENGLISH-JAPANESE INDEX

BEGINNER'S JAPANESE

O
October jūgatsu 13
of course mochiron 132
often yoku 134
oh ā 20
Oh, that's right ā, sō sō 90
OK, all right daijōbu 100
old (things, not people) furui(i) 64
older brother (humble) ani 167
older brother onii-san 40
older sister (humble) ane 167
older sister onē-san 40
once ikkai 82
one ichi 4
one billion jūoku 157
one day ichinichi 82
one hundred hyaku 6
one hundred billion senoku 157
one hundred million ichioku 157
one hundred thousand jūman 157
one million hyakuman 157
one minute ippun 73
one month hitotsuki 82
one month ikkagetsu 8
one month tsuki 82
one month's time tsuki 84
one person hitori 146

one thousand sen 13
one trillion itchō 157
one week isshū 82
one week isshūkan 82
one year ichinen 64
one year old issai 169
one's junior kōhai 92
one's senior sempai 92
only dake 120
open hiraku(-u) 200
operation shujutsu 248
or ka 200
orange orenji (iro) 50
other betsu-no 120
other hoka-no 54
out or away from home rusu(-u) 156
out, outside soto 22
over there asoko 46
overseas kaigai 222
overtime (at work) zangyō 112

P
p.m. gogo 4
package, parcel kozutsumi 178
page pēji 202
pain itami 244
pain, hurt itai 248
pants zubon 16
paper kami 20
parent (polite) oyago-san 167

parents (humble) ryōshin 167
parents (polite) go-ryōshin 167
parking lot chūshajō 188
part-time job arubaito 188
party pātī 6
pay harau(-u) 176
pay tsuku(-u) 204
pen pen 14
pencil enpitsu 20
percent pāsento 202
perhaps tabun 112
person hito 36
person (polite) kata 36
personnel jinji-bu 228
Ph.D. hakushi 114
pharmacy kusuriya 48
pharmacy yakkyoku 48
physical examination kenkō shindan 248
picture shashin 124
picture e 176
picture post card ehagaki 176
pillow makura 166
pinch hasamaru(-u) 244
place tokoro 56
plan tsumori 192
plans, schedule yotei 156
platform hōmu 188
play asobu(-u) 62

284

Track List for Audio CDs

Disc One

1. Pronunciation
2. Lesson One: Dialogue I
3. Lesson One: Dialogue II
4. Lesson One Vocabulary
5. Lesson One: The Numbers 1-12
6. Lesson Two: Dialogue
7. Lesson Two: Vocabulary and Clothes
8. Lesson Two: The Days of the Week
9. Lesson Three: Dialogue I
10. Lesson Three: Dialogue II
11. Lesson Three: Vocabulary, Prepositions, and Common Expressions
12. Lesson Four: Dialogue
13. Lesson Four: Vocabulary and Verbs
14. Lesson Five: Dialogue I
15. Lesson Five: Dialogue II
16. Lesson Five: Vocabulary and Family Terms
17. Lesson Six: Dialogue I
18. Lesson Six: Dialogue II
19. Lesson Six: Vocabulary, Places, and Colors
20. Lesson Seven: Dialogue I
21. Lesson Seven: Dialogue II
22. Lesson Seven: Vocabulary and Food
23. Lesson Eight: Dialogue I
24. Lesson Eight: Dialogue II
25. Lesson Eight: Verbs and Additional Words
26. Lesson Nine: Dialogue I
27. Lesson Nine: Dialogue II
28. Lesson Nine: Vocabulary
29. Lesson Ten: Dialogue I
30. Lesson Ten: Dialogue II
31. Lesson Ten: Vocabulary
32. Lesson Eleven: Dialogue I
33. Lesson Eleven: Dialogue II
34. Lesson Eleven: Vocabulary
35. Lesson Twelve: Dialogue I
36. Lesson Twelve: Dialogue II
37. Lesson Twelve: Vocabulary

Disc Two